CW00735292

2024
Tarot Diary

WWW.KATEMAY.CO.UK

Tarot Diary
2024

Kate May Modern Day Mystic

This diary belongs to

_____

1 - Copyright
2 - Numerology year 8 and Tarot cards
4 - Birth year number with birth Tarot card
5 - Manifest your year with Tarot and numerology
7 - 10 things you are welcoming for 2024
8 - Tarot card energy
9 - Your goals with Tarot and manifesting for 2024
10 - Setting goals for 2024
11 - Monthly goals for 2024
13 - How to use the diary
14 - Tarot cards made easy Major Arcana
16 - Tarot cards made easy Minor Arcana
17 - Tarot cards Major Arcana daily guide
21 - Minor Arcana made easy guide
23 - Suits made easy guide
24 - Court cards made easy
26 - Astrology made easy
27 - New Moon Tarot spread
28 - New Moon Tarot spread
29 - Monthly Tarot spread
30 - Weekly Tarot Spread
31 - Daily Tarot spread
32 - Manifestation Tarot Spread
33 - New year Tarot spread
34 - January Tarot spread
35 - This week's Tarot Vibes week 1
36 - Diary week 1
37 - This week's tarot vibes week 2
38 - Diary week 2
39 - This week's Tarot vibes week 3
40 - Diary week 3
41 - This week's Tarot vibes week 4
42 - Diary week 4
43 - February Tarot spread
44 - Imbolc Tarot Spread
45 - Valentine's day Tarot spread
46 - This week's Tarot vibes week 5
47 - Diary week 5
48 - This week's Tarot vibes week 6
49 - Diary week 6
50 - This week's Tarot vibes week 7
51 - Diary week 7
52 - This week's Tarot vibes week 8
52 - Diary week 8
52 - This week's Tarot vibes week 9
53- Diary week 9
54 - March Tarot spread

55 - Spring Equinox Tarot spread
56 - St Patricks day Tarot Spread
57- St Georges day Tarot spread
58 - This week's Tarot vibes week 10
59 - Diary week 10
60 - This week's Tarot vibes week 11
61- Diary week 11
62 - This week's Tarot vibes week 12
63 - diary week 12
64 -This week's Tarot vibes week 13
65 - Diary weeks 13
66 - This week Tarot vibes week 14
67 - Diary week 14
68 - April Tarot spread
69 - Hot cross bun Tarot spread
70 - Ester/Ostara Tarot spread
71 -This week's Tarot vibes week 15
72 - Diary week 15
73 - This week's Tarot vibes week 16
74 - Diary week 16
75 - This week's Tarot vibes week 17
76 - Diary week 17
77 - This week's Tarot vibes week 18
78 - Diary week 18
79 - May Tarot spread
80 - Beltane Tarot spread
81 - This week's Tarot vibes week 19
82- Diary week 19
83 - This week Tarot vibes week 20
84 - Diary week 20
85 - This week's Tarot vibes week 21
86 - Diary week 21
87 - This week's Tarot vibes week 22
88 - Diary week 22
89 - June Tarot Spread
90 - Summer Solstice Tarot spread
91 - Mid Summer Tarot spread
92 – This week's tarot vibes week 23
93 - Diary week 23
94- This weeks Tarot vibes week 24
95 - Diary week 24
96 - This week's Tarot vibes week 25
97 - Diary week 25
98 - This week's Tarot vibes week 26
99 - Diary week 26
100 - This week's Tarot vibes week 27
101 - Diary week 27

102 - July tarot spread

103 - Summer Tarot spread

104 - This weeks Tarot vibes week 28

105 - Diary week 28

106 - This week Tarot vibes week 29

107- Diary week 29

108 - This week's Tarot vibes week 30

109 - Diary week 30

110 - This week's Tarot vibes week 31

111 - Diary week 31

112 - August Tarot spread

113 - Lammas Tarot spread

114 - This week's Tarot vibe week 32

115 - Diary week 32

116 - This week's Tarot vibes week 33

117 - Diary vibes week 33

118 - This week's Tarot vibes week 34

119 - Diary week 34

120 - This week's Tarot vibes week 35

121 - Diary week 35

122 - September Spread

123 - Autumn Equinox spread

124 - This week's Tarot vibes week 36

125 - Diary week 36

126 - This week's Tarot vibes week 37

127 - Diary week 37

128 - This week's Tarot vibes week 38

129 - Diary week 38

130 - This week's Tarot vibes week 39

131 - Diary week 39

132- This week's Tarot vibes week 40

133 - Diary week 40

134 - October Tarot spread

135 - Halloween/Samhain tarot spread

136 - Witchy Tarot spread

137 - This week's Tarot vibes week 41

138 - Diary week 41

139 - This week's Tarot vibes week 42

140 - Diary week 42

141- This week's Tarot vibes week 43

142 - Diary week 43

143 - This week's Tarot vibes 44

144 - Diary week 44

145- November Tarot spread

146- Fire work Tarot spread

147 - Thanksgiving Tarot spread

148 - This week's Tarot vibes week 45

149 - Diary week 45
150 - This week's Tarot vibes week 46
151 - Diary week 46
152 - This week's Tarot vibes week 47
153 - Diary week 47
154 - This week's Tarot vibes week 48
155 - Diary week 48
156 - December Tarot spread
157 - Winter Solstice Tarot spread
158 - Christmas/yule Tarot spread
159 - This week's Tarot vibes week 49
160 - Diary week 49
161 - This week's Tarot vibes week 50
162 - Diary week 50
163 - This week's Tarot vibes week 51
164 - Diary week 51
165 - This week's Tarot vibes week 52
166 - Diary week 52
167 - This week's Tarot vibes week 53
168 - Diary week 53
169 - This week's tarot vibes week 54
170 - Diary week 54
171- Extras Numerology

2024 is a big year!
In numerology it is the number 8

As the stars align and the celestial energies stir, the year 2024 beckons with a promise of transformation. In the realm of numerology, it bears the mark of the number 8, a symbol of prosperity and movement. Like a wheel that turns and cycles, 8's bring forth power, energy, and courage, paving the way for progress and revolution.

In the mystical realm of Tarot, the 8's hold a pivotal role, embodying the essence of Strength and the Star. For when love triumphs over hate, and one approaches life's challenges with a gentle hand, the strength within is magnified. And as hope glimmers in the distance, illuminating a path to a brighter future, the Star reminds us to hold onto optimism and let its light guide our way.

As the year 2024 unfolds, the magic of Tarot and numerology intertwine, bringing forth the qualities of authority, self-confidence, and inner wisdom. With a love for humanity and a desire for peace, this year promises to be a beacon of success, especially in the realm of business.
Let us then embrace the wonder of this mystical manifestation, and venture forth into the unknown with a heart full of hope and a spirit of adventure.

Your annual tarot card, is going to be one of the major 22 in the tarot deck, encapsulating the essence of your year's voyage. It echoes the rhythm of the path you've chosen, guiding your actions with its mysterious energy. Its enchantment radiates throughout all aspects of the upcoming year, shaping its foundational character through its celestial influence. Hidden within its enigmatic interpretations are threads of guidance, a communication crafted from the threads of destiny. Pay heed, for the yearly tarot card serves as your guide for the year 2024, offering insights and wisdom for your journey ahead.

The mystical essence of your Tarot year can be unlocked by weaving together the strands of your birth day and month with the grand arrival of the new year.

We explore the magic of numbers to gain insights into your destiny for the year 2024. By adding the digits of your birth date, For Example: 09 and 05, to the year 2024, we arrive at the number 22, which is beyond the mystical threshold of 21. Further summing 2 and 2, we arrive at the number 4, representing the Emperor. The Emperor signifies a year of strength and recognition. In 2024, the stars foretell a time of significant growth and opportunities. As you stand in your authoritative position, the spark of inspiration will ignite a vision of the future. This year holds the potential for you to manifest your most ambitious goals, whether you act as a teacher, leader, or mentor. As you navigate through this enchanted year, the magic of respect, structure, and well-defined boundaries will weave a tapestry of success. Allow the wisdom of numbers to guide you on your journey toward your destined path.

Your Tarot birth card is a reflection of your innate qualities, inner desires, and the energies that shape your life. It unveils the mysterious and profound layers of your personality, offering insights into your strengths, weaknesses, and the fundamental forces that drive you. This card also provides a unique perspective on the purpose and direction of your life's journey.

Calculate your birth card, by adding your birth numbers.

First, sum the numbers of your birthdate. For example: 0 + 9 + 0 + 5 + 1 + 9 + 7 + 5 = 36. Since this result is above 21, it is necessary to further reduce it to a single digit. Therefore, add 3 + 6 to obtain the final digit, which is 9.
In this case, the Tarot card associated with the number 9 is "The Hermit." The Hermit card signifies a path of self-discovery, spiritual exploration, and personal journeying. It does not imply a life of perpetual solitude or singularity but, instead, suggests that profound learning is derived from moments of introspection and solitude, rather than exclusively in group settings. Taking time for self-reflection and introspection is deemed essential for your overall well-being.

2024 Use this Tarot Diary To Manifest Your Best Year!

Tarot, an ancient divination system comprised of a deck of symbolic cards, serves multiple purposes beyond the mere interpretation of esoteric symbols. While its primary function is often regarded as a means to gain insight, seek clarification, and receive guidance, it also possesses the unique capacity to function as a tool for manifestation.

Tarot's ability to provide insight is rooted in its rich symbolism and archetypal imagery, which enables individuals to tap into their subconscious thoughts and emotions. By laying out and interpreting the cards, one can gain valuable insights into personal challenges, relationships, and potential pathways forward. The act of consulting the Tarot is akin to opening a door to one's inner world, inviting a deeper understanding of the self and the circumstances at hand.

Additionally, Tarot offers a platform for clarification, allowing individuals to refine their thoughts and intentions. When faced with complex decisions or dilemmas, the process of drawing and contemplating Tarot cards can illuminate previously overlooked facets of a situation, fostering greater clarity and purpose in decision-making.

Furthermore, Tarot can be employed as a potent guidance tool. The cards serve as a source of wisdom, offering perspectives and advice that can be instrumental in navigating life's challenges. Tarot readings, conducted with sincerity and an open mind, provide a source of counsel and direction, aiding individuals in making informed choices and taking decisive actions.

Beyond these conventional uses, Tarot possesses the intriguing capability to function as a manifestation tool. Through the focused intent and visualisation of desired outcomes while using the Tarot, individuals can align their energies and intentions with the symbolism of the cards. This practice can empower individuals to manifest their goals and aspirations, leveraging the Tarot as a conduit for self-empowerment and the realisation of their dreams.

Ten things you are welcoming for 2024

1 _____

2 _____

3 _____

4 _____

5 _____

6 _____

7 _____

8 _____

9 _____

10 _____

Tarot Cards Energy

Each Tarot card possesses distinct and symbolic energies, making them a potent resource for the practice of manifestation magic. The rich symbolism and inherent meanings within the Tarot can be systematically employed to align one's intentions with the forces at play in the universe, facilitating the realisation of desired outcomes.

Examples:

Financial area - The Ace of pentacles, 9 of pentacles, 10 of pentacles
Moving house - Chariot - 9 of pentacles
New love - Ace of cups, 2 of cups or The Lovers
Confidence to manifest - The Magician
Improve your psychic ability - The High priestess
Overcoming challenges - The Chariot
To bring more opportunities your way - 8 of wands

Utilise these energies to facilitate the materialisation of your desires. Commence by meditating upon and forming a connection with them. On auspicious occasions like new or full moons or whenever an inner prompting arises, incorporate your selected card or cards into your sacred space, alongside specific crystals, herbs, or any other components, to initiate the process of manifesting your intentions consider your aspirations at multiple temporal levels, including your weekly, monthly, and yearly objectives

Establishing a clear goal serves as the foundation for setting your intentions and concentration. I encourage you to allocate some time for contemplation, reflecting upon the objectives you wish to achieve and the specific manifestations you seek to bring into existence. It is advisable to give thought to the various facets of your goals, exploring the different areas and dimensions they encompass.

Your Goals

Goal for the coming year in my relationship area is ....

_____

My goal for the coming year in my Finance area is....

_____

My goal for the coming year in my Finance area is....

_____

My goal for the coming year in my Health area is ....

_____

My goal for the coming year in my Family area is ....

_____

My goal for the coming year in my Career area is ....

_____

The process of setting goals initiates a powerful intention that echoes across the universe. It signifies your willingness to embark on a transformative journey.

To navigate this path with ease, it's essential to divide each goal into manageable fragments of time, taking one step at a time to prevent being inundated with feelings of being overwhelmed. It is important to acknowledge that some pursuits may take longer than others. Therefore, in your pursuit, be compassionate towards yourself and create a realistic yet enchanting tapestry.

Monthly Goals

January Goals

February Goals

March Goals

April Goals

May Goals

June Goals

Monthly Goals

July Goals

August Goals

September Goals

October Goals

November Goals

December Goals

Welcome to your Tarot diary 2024.

I've created this diary to serve not only as a weekly planner for the upcoming year but also as a potent tool for tarot manifestation. I've included various tarot spreads designed for different months and occasions, offering you the chance to explore a wide range of themes throughout the year.

This diary also provides your tarot numerology year number and its corresponding message. I've explained how to calculate your personal year number and included a unique birth number, along with its calculation and the corresponding tarot card. To make the most of your daily practice, I've included methods for using the cards in alignment with astrology and manifestation techniques that correspond to each week's tarot cards.

Furthermore, I've dedicated journaling space for you to record your manifestation goals and progress. The diary features easy-to-understand tarot and astrology pages to help you gain a deeper understanding of these mystical arts and how to harness their power for manifesting your desires. This diary is a comprehensive guide designed to empower you on your journey of self-discovery and personal growth

The Fool - The start of a new chapter. Beginnings. Jouneys

The Magician - Manifestation. Confidence. Raw power.

The High Priestess - Secrets. Intuition. Psychic abilities. Inner knowing,

The Empress - Abundance. Fertility. Mother. Mother Earth. Loving.

The Emperor - Foundations. Father figure. Boundaries. Firm but fair.

The Hiraphant - Beliefs. Tradition. Education. Groups and communities.

The Lovers - Communication. Choices. Soul mates.

Strength - Love wins over hate. Tact. Gentle strength.

The Chariot - Overcoming obstacles. Home coming. Determination. Focus.

Hermit - Reflection. Introspection. Time out. Solitude.

Wheel of fortune - Luck. Change. Destiny. Movement

Justice - Truth. Accountability. Legalities.

Hanged Man - Seeing things from a different perspective. Hanging around. Sacrifice.

Death - Change. Endings. Transition.

Temperance - Balance. Patience. Harmony.Travel.

The Devil - Toxicity. Choices. Temptation, Unhealthy behaviour.

The Tower - Destruction. Chaos. Breaking old ways. Unexpected change

The star - Sparkle of light. Hope. Optimism. New dawn.

Moon - Emotions. Intuition. All is not as it seems

The Sun - Fun. Freedom. Inner child. Happy families.

Judgement - Awakening. Release. Understanding. Decisions. Transition.

The World - New chapter. Travel. Full Circle.

One - New Beginnings, potential, opportunity -
Fool/Magician

Two - Choices, balance, duality - The High Priestess/Justice
Judgement

Three - Teams, small groups, milestones, growth, relationships
The Empress/The Hanged Man/The world

Four - Foundations, security, structure, stability, planning
The Emperor/Death

Five - Challenges and conflicts - The
Hierophant/Temperance

Six - Choices, compassion, harmony - The Lovers/The
Devil

Seven - Reevaluating, Weighing up situations, reflection,
understanding
The Chariot/The Tower

Eight - Opportunities, movement, attainment, pivotal position
Strength/The Star

Nine - Near completion, fruition ,fulfilment, Pause - The
Hermit/The moon

Ten - Completion, end of cycle, transformation - Wheel of
fortune/The Sun

Fool: Consider taking a calculated risk, embarking on an adventure, or trying something novel. Embrace the idea of being open to vulnerability as you explore new opportunities. It's through these bold actions that you may discover uncharted territories and potentially unlock valuable experiences and growth.

Magician: Manifestation at its peak. The realm of possibilities is wide open, and anything you aspire to achieve can become a reality. Seize this day to take action on your dreams and desires, transforming them into tangible and earthly existence. With the right focus, dedication, and effort, you have the power to bring your aspirations to life.

High Priestess: It is essential to place your trust in your intuition. The energies of the day may hold hidden secrets and mysteries. If you sense uncertainty or intrigue, consider delving deeper into your Tarot cards for insight or seek guidance from a psychic or medium. Take the time to meditate and reflect upon anything that leaves you feeling unsure or perplexed. Your intuition and these practices can help you uncover hidden truths and gain a clearer understanding of the situation.

Empress: Presents an excellent opportunity to spend time in nature, connect with Mother Earth, or strengthen bonds with your family. Consider indulging in a pamper day that nourishes your well-being. Remember that nurturing what you want to cultivate is essential. Take this time to recharge, reflect, and invest in the aspects of your life that you wish to see flourish and thrive.

Emperor: Father figures may hold significance. It's essential to establish clear boundaries and maintain a strong sense of self. This is a favorable day for activities related to promotions and engaging in the public speaking sector. Approach your interactions with a balance of firmness and fairness, ensuring that you assert your authority when needed while upholding a sense of justice and equity.

The Hiraphant: *It* is advisable not to disrupt the status quo or make abrupt changes today. Adhering to routine and following established rules and regulations will be in your favor. Additionally, seeking counsel or advice within your spiritual beliefs can bring valuable insights and knowledge. Embracing the stability of familiar practices and consulting spiritual guidance will contribute to your wisdom and well-being.

Lovers: Choices that have an impact on others, particularly within the realm of romance or relationships, should be treated with utmost importance today. When it comes to a strong connection between two individuals, open and honest communication is paramount. Ensuring that your interactions are characterised by transparency and understanding will be essential to maintaining and nurturing these valuable connections.

Chariot: Presents an opportunity for you to exercise self-control and remain focused without allowing distractions to sway you. Stay committed to your path and avoid veering off course. This resolute approach is likely to lead to a victorious outcome or a positive homecoming that will bring about favorable effects and results.

Strength: Exercise restraint with your words today. You may find it necessary to hold your tongue and summon your inner strength to navigate challenging situations. Keep in mind that love and understanding are more potent than hatred or anger. Embracing a compassionate and composed approach can help you effectively address and resolve difficult circumstances.

Hermit: Today is a day for reflection and introspection. Allocate some time to turn your focus inward. Meditation can be particularly beneficial, offering spiritual guidance and wisdom. By taking this opportunity for introspection, you can gain valuable insights and enhance your sense of inner peace and clarity.

Wheel of Fortune: Consider making a change to propel progress and be willing to take a chance. Today, it appears that Lady Luck is on your side. Seize the opportunity to embrace change and take calculated risks, as they may lead to favorable outcomes and advancements.

Justice: **It is crucial to ensure that you remain on the right side of the law and truth today. There is a possibility that final outcomes will be resolved in legal matters or, at the very least, a decision will be reached that will contribute to the ultimate resolution of these issues. It's essential to uphold legal and ethical standards while navigating any legal proceedings, as the decisions made can have significant consequences.**

The Hanged Man: **You will need to adopt a different perspective, one that prioritises making sacrifices for a long-term visio. This might involve letting go of what is currently holding you back, even if it feels difficult or uncomfortable. Such sacrifices can lead to greater progress and achievement of your long-term goals.**

Death: **There are endings or changes afoot today. It's a pertinent time to consider what needs to come to an end in your life. Reflect on areas where change is necessary. It's important to recognise that before something new can commence, there must be an ending or a closure to set the stage for fresh beginnings and progress. Evaluate where it's time to conclude one chapter to pave the way for the next.**

Temperance: **Be prepared for the possibility that your patience may be put to the test today. Maintain your composure and balance, keeping one foot firmly grounded to navigate any challenges. This could be a favorable day for delving into philosophical or spiritual research, exploring questions related to the meaning of life. Take this opportunity to seek understanding and insight into the profound aspects of existence.**

Devil: **It is worth considering how blocks, setbacks, and restrictions might affect your sense of freedom. However, it's essential to remember that you still have choices in how you respond to these challenges. You can choose to release what is holding you back or consuming your energy. Be cautious about committing to things without careful consideration, as unhealthy temptations may appear alluring today. Be mindful of the choices you make and the potential consequences they may carry.**

Tower: Brace yourself for a day filled with unexpected surprises and potential chaos. Embrace these shifts as the universe's way of indicating that something was not secure enough and requires rebuilding. While it may be unsettling, these changes can ultimately lead to a stronger and more stable foundation. Be adaptable and open to the transformations that come your way, as they may bring valuable opportunities for growth and improvement.

Star: Today is a positive day where hope and optimism reign supreme. Fresh hope and renewal arrive through new experiences and opportunities. The energy around you is starting to align harmoniously and in perfect synchrony. Embrace this sense of optimism and use it to move forward with confidence and enthusiasm.

Moon: It is imperative to extend kindness to yourself today. Emotions may fluctuate, and the energy around you may be changeable and perplexing. It is advisable to exercise patience and refrain from making significant decisions until the situation becomes clearer. Additionally, pay attention to your dreams tonight, as they might hold valuable insights and guidance during this period of emotional variability.

Sun: Today is an excellent day to devote time to your family. Reconnect with your inner child and engage in enjoyable activities together. Embrace the opportunity for fun and bonding with your loved ones, as it can create precious memories and strengthen your relationships.

Judgement: Today may bring about a realisation that has the potential to transform your entire perspective. It's important to exercise caution in making judgments, whether they concern others or even yourself. The insights gained could challenge preconceived notions and lead to a deeper understanding of the complexities of the situation. Be open to the possibility of a profound shift in your awareness and attitudes.

The World: Today presents an excellent opportunity to plan a vacation or contemplate your next venture. Consider taking steps to wrap up any remaining loose ends, preparing for the start of a new and exciting chapter in your journey. Whether it's a well-deserved break or a fresh business endeavor, this is a favorable time for forward-thinking and preparation.

Ace's in Tarot

The Ace position holds the boundless energy that exists before creation. The Potential is limitless. The door is unlocked and ready to open. Where you go next is entirely up to you. A new opportunity, the conception awaits.

Two's in Tarot

The two's position brings us unions and togetherness. As we move from One to Two, from single to double, we see partnership and harmony. Twos can symbolize the beauty of relationships, duality and opposition, even the potential for creation. Bringing two people together in harmony, being on the same page.

Three's in Tarot

The three's form from the Two's potential for creation, and partnerships comes the Three. The Three cards represent development and creativity. Reaching a milestone. They bring the next part of a journey but with collaboration, teamwork or where three induvial are connected in this next stage in order to progress forward
.

Four's in Tarot

The Four's bring us the completion of the Three's creating, the firm foundation for the next chapter. Fours represent stability, success and a strong base upon which upon to build, bringing the realisation that our work is not yet finished. They can also indicate the need to take a period of rest before moving forward again.

Five's inTarot

The five's job is to continue building towards our goals, despite some challenges perhaps from the early structures, often unstable, leading us to necessary conflict and struggles, as we fight to keep stability. As everything this phase does pass.

Six's in Tarot

After the chaos of the Fives, the Sixes represent the calm movement to restore balance, and realignment to the building once more. They bring peace and act as the bridge between the challenges of the past and the hope for the future. The Sixes bring our awareness for the need to let go, leaving the troubles behind and pointing us back on track. Another milestone is reached, pleasing those that are around us.

Seven's in Tarot

The Sevens bring us into a re-evaluation period, the need for patience and perseverance. We see the lessons we have learned over time, and with that patience and stamina we continue our growth realising how far our efforts have taken us as we move on to the next phase.

Eight's in Tarot

The Eights indicate a change of pace, with a time of profound but positive change. Our roles are shifting, we are more secure and focused on our desires and goals, we have established systems and foundations that support us. We are nearing the conclusions, but we still have further work to do. Effort and detail pay important factors as we take all opportunities to master our tasks and move forward.

Nine's in Tarot

When Nines appear, we are nearing the completion of our work or phase, the final milestone is in sight, and we can have a moment of pause before we do a final push toward the finish line. We feel proud and happy knowing that the hard work we have endured has been worth it and seen such growth.

Ten's in Tarot

The Tens indicate the end of a cycle, a change of direction, the outcome. Mentally, physically and spiritually. Moving from one phase of our lives to another in a brand-new cycle. This full journey can see us feeling depleted, exhausted at time, taking time to rest before moving forward again may be necessary.

In the 56 cards of the Minor Arcana, there are four suits, based on the elements and seasons. Fire, Water, Air, Earth. Spring Summer, Autumn and Winter.
Each suit is made up of 14 cards Ace to Ten and then the court Cards Page, Knight, Queen and King.

Suit of Wands: **Action (Fire) Aries, Leo, Sagittarius. Spring time.**
The suit of Wands corrospond to our soul's action, movement, and growth. Wands in a reading prompt us to look at how we move through our life. What sparks our desires and drives us to reach our goals, and find our purpose. Can also relate to travel.

Suit of Cups: **Emotional (Water) Cancer, Scorpio, Pisces. Summer Time.**
The suit of Cups relates to our emotions and matters of the heart. Cups in a reading are associated with love, feelings, and inner conflict, our relationships and spiritual endeavours. They ask us to feel what is deeply important to us in our hearts and souls. Relates also to our intuition.

Suit of Swords: **Mental (Air) Gemini, Libra, Aquarius. Autumn Time.**
The suit of Swords is connected with the mind. Specifically, it focuses on the mind's decisive capabilities. Swords in a reading can indicate the need to make a decision, be it difficult or clear. Can also relate our mental state of mind and well being.

Suit of Pentacles: **Physical (Earth) Taurus, Virgo, Capricorn. Winter time.**
The suit of Pentacles is connected to the material or physical world. Pentacles in a reading can relate to situations about money, resources, property and levels of success and prosperity. Also connected to our physical self.

Within the ancient deck of mystical wisdom, the pages unveil a narrative of beginnings in their embryonic form. Their youthful vitality serves as a radiant beacon, illuminating uncharted pathways and budding concepts. They move with the exuberance of those unburdened by the weight of age, their presence heralding novelty and renewal.

Yet, their influence transcends youth, for the pages have the power to invoke the spirits of those young at heart or those awakening to fresh horizons. With their arrival, the seeds of potential are sown, awaiting the gentle touch of time and nurturing to flourish.

As the pages announce the emergence of fresh starts, the knights charge forth, wielding the force of action. Armed with a sense of maturity and purpose, they embrace the pages' nascent ideas and set out to bring them to fruition. They embody dynamism, serving as the sparks that set the wheel of progress in motion. Although they may not possess the wisdom of the king or the nurturing compassion of the queen, the knights are formidable catalysts for change, manifesting the pages' initial spark.

The Queens, both in the context of an individual and as an event, embody a stage of life or soul that is slightly more advanced, typically reflecting a person in their 40s or someone who possesses a deeper understanding of themselves and their surroundings. These individuals are marked by their wisdom and experience, having acquired insights through their life journeythey often represent the feminine aspects, their characteristics can manifest in any gender. The Queens exude a nurturing aura, akin to a maternal or elder sisterly presence,[24] and they are inclined to offer support and guidance to aid others in their personal growth.

When these cards appear in a reading, they prompt you to delve into the symbolic elements associated with the card, but on a more mature and sensitive level. The Queens are distinguished by their superior wisdom compared to the Knights and possess the know-how to nurture and foster growth. To draw a metaphor, think of the Queen as the one who waters the seed that has already been planted.

The Kings, on the other hand, represent individuals who would typically be in their 50s or older. They stand as paragons of experience and expertise, offering valuable advice and guidance. These mature figures possess a wealth of knowledge and speak with authority and credibility. Among the court cards, the Kings are the most seasoned, demonstrating mastery in their respective domains. They exhibit a high degree of self-control across all aspects of life and tend to assert control in their interactions with others and their approach to various situations.

In a broader context, when Kings appear in a reading, they shed light on the best methods for handling a given situation, advocating the need for taking control or seeking counsel from a knowledgeable and experienced source. The King cards are particularly useful in foreseeing the ultimate outcomes of situations. They can be likened to the final blossom of a flower, representing the culmination of efforts and experiences.

To draw an analogy, consider the Page as a seed, a fledgling entity brimming with potential. With proper care and guidance, it matures into the Knight, where ideas or individuals take action and are planted to grow into their full potential. The nurturing and care bestowed upon the seed equate to the influence of the Queens, who help it flourish. Ultimately, this loving attention brings the seed to its zenith, transforming it into the King, fully realiSed and ready for the world.

Venus: Love - Emotions, beauty, sensuality, Finance, Value, Security, Pleasure

Moon: Intuition - sensitivity, mood, hidden things, emotional changes

Uranus: Intellect - Uncontrollable events, change, social justice, freedom

Pluto: Sex - Change, death, rebirth, transformation

Neptune: Spirituality, loss, confusion, where spirituality can help you through loss

Mercury : Communication,learning, technology,intelligence

Jupiter: Luck - Expansion, success, achievements

Sun: Self - Ego, vitality ,expression, life force.

Mars: Power - Force, aggression, sex, energy

Saturn: Restriction - Limitations, control, happiness

New Moon Tarot Spread

1
2 4
3

*New Moon energy vibe
*How can you manifest your ideas now
*What area needs your focus on at this time
*New moon tarot message

Full Moon Tarot Spread

1

5

2

4

3

*Full Moon energy
*What is being highlighted
*No longer serves you
*How can you release this?
*Emotionally how you can find balance

Monthly Tarot Spread

*This months main vibe
*How can you support this vibe
*Lessons
*Opportunities
*Reflection
*Monthly tarot message

Weekly Tarot Spread

1   2   5

4   3   6

*This weeks main vibe
*How can you support this vibe
*Lessons to learn this week
*Opportunities coming to you
this week

Daily Tarot Spread

Kate May Modern Day Mystic

2

1

3

4

*What is today's tarot guidance
*How can you support your energy
today
*How can you embrace today's lessons
*Today's purpose

Manifestation Tarot Spread

*Manifestations energy

*Route to achieve desires

*What do you need to do to make the first step

*Blocks to over come

*Positive energy to achieve your manifestation

New Year Tarot Spread

*What lessons are there from the previous year
*New focus for the coming year
*Blessings to celebrate
*Guidance to overcome any challenges
*Finances for the next year
*Health for the next year
*Career for the next year
*Positive new year message

January
Tarot Spread

1	4
2	5
3	6

*January Vibe
*New Hopes
* Action needed
*Challenge to overcome
*Liight to come
*Tarot message

This Weeks Tarot Vibes

Tarot: 3 of Pentacles -1-8th January - Astrology: Mars in Capricorn

In the coming week, the alignment of tarot and astrology suggests a strong emphasis on teamwork and collaboration. Working with others will be the key to achieving success during this period. This combination of energies is driving and powerful, encouraging you to focus on your goals and projects. It's an excellent time to put your efforts into long-term objectives and significant tasks.

Building practical bonds with your colleagues and peers will be particularly beneficial, as this teamwork-oriented approach will help you make substantial progress. As you work together, you can form the foundation for your future goals and aspirations. So, embrace collaboration, set your sights on your ambitions, and make the most of the productive energy surrounding you this week.

Mystic Message:
Certainly, to achieve success, it is essential to utilize all available and supported resources. This includes leveraging your skills, knowledge, tools, and the assistance of others when necessary. By making the most of these resources, you can enhance your chances of reaching your goals and attaining success. Be proactive in seeking out and utilising the resources at your disposal to ensure you're well-prepared and equipped for the tasks ahead.

Manifesting:
When manifesting with the Three of Pentacles, you are focusing on building working relationships, fostering friendships, and encouraging collaborations. This card is especially auspicious when you are seeking to bring people with various skills and talents together for a common goal or project.

January   week 1

1 **Monday**
3 of pentacles

---

2 **Tuesday**
3 of pentacles

---

3 **Wednesday**
3 of pentacles

---

4 **Thursday**
3 of pentacles

---

5 **Friday**
3 of pentacles

---

6 **Saturday**
3 of pentacles

---

7 **Sunday**
3 of pentacles

This Weeks Tarot Vibes

Tarot: 4 of pentacles 9th - 15th January - Astrology: Sun in Capricorn

Be mindful of your cash flow this week. I suggests that you should manage your finances carefully, but not to the extent that it restricts the flow of resources. encourage yourself to reconsider your financial and material handling strategies and assess whether you are flexible enough to adapt if necessary.

The Tarot and Astrology combination highlights the importance of balancing hard work and fun in your life. It warns against excessive focus on work, which can lead to boredom or becoming boring. It emphasises that too much emphasis on work can result in stagnation and rigidity.

Mystic message:
Reinforces the idea of balance and cautions against being overly cautious to the point of getting stuck. It encourages you to keep things balanced in your life for the best results, suggesting that a balanced approach will lead to better outcomes.

Manifesting:
With the 4 of Pentacles, this card symbolises a situation where you are endeavoring to save money for a specific goal, despite the temptation to indulge in spending. Using this card in a positive manner involves exercising caution and diligently working towards your financial security. It advises you to stay focused on your financial objectives and resist impulsive spending to achieve your desired level of financial stability.

January   Week 2

8 **Monday**
4 of pentacles

9 **Tuesday**
4 of pentacles

10 **Wednesday**
4 of pentacles

11 **Thursday**
4 of pentacles

12 **Friday**
4 of pentacles

13 **Saturday**
4 of pentacles

14 **Sunday**
4 of pentacles

Tarot: 4 of pentacles - 16th -19th January - Astrology:
Sun in Capricorn
Tarot: 5 of Swords - 20th - 22nd January - Astrology:
Venus in Aquarius

Exercise prudence when it comes to your financial
expenditures this week. It's imperative to assess the
true value of a victory, as some battles may not be
worth the effort, while others unquestionably are.
In the realm of Tarot and Astrology, the Sun's transit
through Capricorn carries a somber undertone. It
necessitates quick thinking and the application of
practicality to surmount any challenges that may arise.

Mystic message:
In instances of a mental conflict or internal struggle, it
is advisable to allocate time for examining the
situation from an alternative perspective.

Manifesting:
On a positive note, it is advisable to promote open
communication and astute thinking when seeking
assistance and support to navigate challenging
situations and find solutions to your predicaments.

January week 3

15 **Monday**
4 of pentacles

16 **Tuesday**
4 of pentacles

17 **Wednesday**
4 of pentacles

18 **Thursday**
4 of pentacles

19 **Friday**
4 of pentacles

20 **Saturday**
5 of swords

21 **Sunday**
5 of swords

This Weeks Tarot Vibes

Tarot: 5 of Swords 23rd - 29th January - Astrology: Venus in Aquarious

Steer clear of conflicts and disharmony throughout this week. It is crucial to carefully evaluate the battles you choose to engage in, if any, and determine whether they are truly worthwhile.
Sometimes, it is wise to distance yourself from unnecessary drama, as short-term losses can often translate into long-term gains. It is essential to assess what will ultimately lead to your long-term happiness and well-being.
In the context of Tarot and Astrology, it's worth noting that there exists a delicate balance between relationships and personal freedom, and this line may become blurred, potentially necessitating challenging decisions.

Mystic message:
Take a moment for introspection and inquire within to discern what truly merits the effort and engagement in a battle.

Manifesting:
Allocate some time for introspection to identify what, or who, is currently sapping your energy and well-being. Then, envision a scenario of serenity and tranquility to replace the draining elements in your life.

January Week 4

22 Monday
5 of swords

23 Tuesday
5 of swords

24 Wednesday
5 of swords

25 Thursday
5 of swords

26 Friday
5 of swords

27 Saturday
5 of swords

28 Sunday
5 of swords

*Pause and reflect
*New ideas forming
*Short comings to over come
*Light on the horizon
*Guidance to support you now

Imbolc Tarot Spread

*What is thawing for you
*New growth that needs your focus
*Hope to come
*Changes for the season
*Imbolc message for you

Valentines Tarot Spread

*Relationship Vibe
*Challenges
*How to deal wth challenges
*Your feelings
*Your partner's feelings
*Good news supporting this relationship
*Potential outcome

This Weeks Tarot Vibes

Tarot: 5 of Swords 29th January - Astrology: Venus in Aquarious
Tarot: 6 of Swords 1-5th February - Astrology: Mercury in Aquarius

This week presents an opportune moment for the contemplation and formulation of travel plans, or for navigating your way out of challenging circumstances. Once a transition occurs, you can expect a smoother, more tranquil trajectory. It's an excellent time to explore new horizons and progress from one stage to the next. When considering the fusion of Tarot and Astrology, Mercury's presence in Aquarius holds the potential for profound life changes. Be unafraid to enact vital transformations, even if it involves stepping outside their comfort zone. Harness this energy to advance in the intricate game of life.

Mystic message:
Place your trust in the process.

Manifesting:
Embrace the transformative energy of the 6 of swords and allow it to guide you on a journey of self-discovery. This card's influence can lead you to more serene and tranquil waters in your life.

February Week 5

29 Monday
5 of swords

---

30 Tuesday
6 of swords

---

31 Wednesday
6 of swords

---

1 Thursday
6 of swords

---

2 Friday
6 of swords

---

3 Saturday
6 of swords

---

4 Sunday
6 of swords

This Weeks Tarot Vibes

Tarot: 6 of Swords - 6-8 February -Astrology: Mercury in Aquarius
Tarot: 7 of Swords 9-11 February - Astrology: Moon in Aquarious

You are persistently progressing towards calmer waters and gaining greater clarity regarding your destination as the week unfolds. However, the latter part of the week brings with it a cautionary note, urging you to exercise discernment in choosing who to trust and who to be cautious of. Remain vigilant when dealing with deceitful individuals, staying one step ahead of their games.
In the context of Tarot and Astrology, it is wise to approach situations with intelligence and mindfulness, avoiding getting entangled in murky or ambiguous circumstances that might lead you away from your initial intentions. Stay focused and resolute in your pursuits.

Mystic message:
Exercise astute judgment, as you possess the wisdom to discern the correct path.

Manifesting:
Permit these cards to serve as your guide in discerning whom to place your trust in and how to make wise decisions instead of impulsive ones.

February week 6

5 **Monday**
5 of swords

6 **Tuesday**
6 of swords

7 **Wednesday**
6 of swords

8 **Thursday**
6 of swords

9 **Friday**
7 of swords

10 **Saturday**
7 of swords

11 **Sunday**
7 of swords

This Weeks Tarot Vibes

Tarot: 7 of Swords 13 -18 February - Astrology: Moon in Aquarius
Tarot: 8 of Cups 19th February - Astrology: Saturn in Pisces

This week, it is of utmost importance to maintain a cautious approach and remain vigilant. There is a possibility that you might encounter deceitful or underhanded actions. I strongly advise against succumbing to the temptation of making questionable decisions.

As we transition into the 8 of cups in the realm of Tarot, we are confronted with a clear message to let go of elements in our lives that have ceased to be beneficial or meaningful.

In the spheres of Tarot and Astrology, there are moments when we all feel the urge to rebel, disregarding the rational inner voice that guides us. It is paramount to embrace your true, authentic self and unapologetically follow your unique path. Place your trust in your intuition to illuminate the correct course of action.

Mystic message:
Maintain your vigilance and caution, as you are on the verge of departing from that which no longer holds value or serves your interests.

Manifesting:
Initiate proactive steps to instigate positive transformations in your life. Utilise the symbolism of the 8 of cups card as a guide to identify the necessary emotional changes.

February Week 8

12 **Monday**
7 of swords

13 **Tuesday**
7 of swords

14 **Wednesday**
7 of swords

15 **Thursday**
7 of swords

16 **Friday**
7 of swords

17 **Saturday**
7 of swords

18 **Sunday**
7 of swords

This Weeks Tarot Vibes

Tarot: 8 of cups - 20th - 26th Febuary Astrology: Saturn in Pisces

This week may prove to be an emotionally charged period as you come to the realisation of what no longer holds value in your life and embark on a new path. It presents an excellent opportunity for deep introspection, meditation, and the exploration of a fresh spiritual perspective. You are gradually aligning yourself with your inherent destiny.

In the context of Tarot and Astrology, a significant shift is underway, bridging the gap between reality and fantasy. The constraints and limitations that have held you back can be lifted, allowing you to pursue your true desires and calling with unwavering dedication. Use this week to lay the groundwork for manifesting your highest purpose.

Mystic Message:
Embark on a journey to discover your true calling and authentic self.

Manifesting:
Engage in meditation focused on this card to cultivate an awareness of your spiritual path, promoting personal growth for your highest well-being.

Febuary week 9

19 Monday
8 of cups

20 Tuesday
8 of cups

21 Wednesday
8 of cups

22 Thursday
8 of cups

23 Friday
8 of cups

24 Saturday
8 of cups

25 Sunday
8 of cups

March Tarot Spread

1

2

3

4

5

6

*This months vibe
*New opportunities awakening
*Something to feel excited about
*Financial news this month
*Health this month
*Tarot message

Spring Equinox Tarot Spread

*What has new potential
*How can you balance your energies
*Hope coming
*Flourishing for you
*What area needs watering now

St Patricks Day
Tarot Spread

3

5

2

4

1

*Luck energy around you
*How can you create more luck
*What luck can you be grateful for
*Lucky money tip
*Lucky tarot message

St George Day Tarot Spread

*Feast for you
*Achievements
*What sacrifices are needed now
*How can you win your battles
*Your dragon message

This Weeks Tarot Vibes

Tarot: 8 of cups 27th - 28th March Astrology: Saturn in Pisces
Tarot 9 of cups 1st - 5th March Astrology: Jupiter in Pisces

Transitioning from the final stages of what no longer serves you, you are progressing towards a state of increased contentment and emotional fulfillment. It is a time to acknowledge and appreciate your blessings, as you become more content and find satisfaction within yourself.
Within the realms of Tarot and Astrology, the removal of emotional and spiritual restrictions is creating an opening for your most significant aspirations to materialise, offering boundless potential for emotional satisfaction and fulfillment.

Mystic message:
It is possible for dreams to become a reality.

Manifesting:
Utilise this card when you aspire to attain a greater sense of inner peace and equilibrium in your life. It serves as a means to foster harmony and a profound feeling of contentment within yourself.

Feb/March week 10

26 **Monday**
8 of cups

27 **Tuesday**
8 of cups

28 **Wednesday**
8 of cups

29 **Thursday**
8 of cups

1 **Friday**
9 of cups

2 **Saturday**
9 of cups

3 **Sunday**
9 of cups

This Weeks Tarot Vibes

Tarot: 9 of cups - 4th - 8th March - Astrology: Jupiter in Pisces
Tarot: 10 of cups - Mars in Pisces Astrology: Jupiter in Pisces and Mars in Pisces

This week offers an excellent opportunity to spend time with family and friends, and it's an ideal occasion to reflect on your blessings. Consider initiating a gratitude journal to capture your appreciation for the positive aspects of your life. The prevailing energy is characterized by happiness, a carefree spirit, and emotional contentment.
In the realms of Tarot and Astrology, the conditions are ripe for manifesting your aspirations and constructing your reality from your dreams and desires. This amalgamation of energies opens the door to limitless possibilities.

Mystic message:
Have the courage to dream, for in doing so, you open the door to infinite possibilities.

Manifesting:
Utilise these cards as a means to foster happiness and harmony within the relationships you share with your family and friends.

March Week 11

4 Monday

9 of cups

---

5 Tuesday

9 of cups

---

6 Wednesday

9 of cups

---

7 Thursday

9 of cups

---

8 Friday

9 of cups

---

9 Saturday

9 of cups

---

10 Sunday

10 of cups

This Weeks Tarot Vibes

Tarot: 10 of cups - 11-17 March - Astrology: Mars in Pisces

This week is a splendid opportunity to cherish moments with your family and friends, savoring success, and relishing a deep sense of emotional satisfaction and contentment. Dedicate time and effort to realize your dreams, as the prevailing energy of the week is conducive to such pursuits.
In the context of Tarot and Astrology, your drive and focus are directed toward enjoying the company of those you hold dear, which, in turn, brings you pleasure and harmony.

Mystic Message:
Indeed, the saying "Home is where the heart is" holds true.

Manifesting:
This approach fosters a harmonious and emotionally fulfilling domestic life, serving to unite and strengthen family bonds.

March Week 12

11 **Monday**
10 of cups

12 **Tuesday**
10 of cups

13 **Wednesday**
10 of cups

14 **Thursday**
10 of cups

15 **Friday**
10 of cups

16 **Saturday**
10 of cups

17 **Sunday**
10 of cups

Tarot: 10 of Cups 18-20th March - Astrology:Mars in Capricorn
Tarot: 21st - 24th 2 of Wands - Astrology: Mars in Aries

In the context of a formal message, your statement can be revised for clarity and professionalism as follows:
"While cultivating a stable domestic environment, you can channel your attention towards your objectives and the promising opportunities that lie ahead. Achieving your goals necessitates proactive effort.
In the realms of Tarot and Astrology, there is a discernible surge of passion and determination propelling you towards the enhancement of your life and the realisation of your ambitions."
This version maintains the essence of your original message while improving its structure and formality.

Mystic message:
"You possess the self-assuredness to advance in your visions.

Manifesting:
"When aspiring for greater achievements in life and yearning for the realization of your goals through tangible actions..."

March Week 13

18 Monday
10 of cups

19 Tuesday
10 of cups

20 Wednesday
10 of cups

21 Thursday
2 of Wands

22 Friday
2 of Wands

23 Saturday
2 of Wands

24 Sunday
2 of Wands

This Weeks Tarot Vibes

Tarot: 2 of Wands - 25th - 28th March -Astrology: Mars in Aries
Tarot: 28th - 31st - 3 of Wands - Astrology: Sun in Aries

This week's energy is brimming with dynamism, significantly influenced by the vigor of Aries. Harness this high energy to your advantage by careful planing and cultivating moments of inspiration. Embrace collaboration and remain receptive to partnerships; achieving positive milestones is well within your reach.
In the realms of Tarot and Astrology, it's important to recognise that action holds the power to create enchanting outcomes. The prevailing abundance of action and fiery energy this week presents an ideal opportunity to set your ambitions in motion.

Mystic message:
We are starting to witness the emergence of outcomes influenced by creative endeavors.

Manifesting:
When aiming to attain greater heights, it is imperative to seek clarity in your actions, especially in the realms of professional work or creative pursuits, in order to achieve successful milestones.

March Week 14

25 Monday
2 of Wands

26 Tuesday
2 of Wands

27 Wednesday
2 of Wands

28 Thursday
2 of Wands

29 Friday
3 of Wands

30 Saturday
3 of Wands

31 Sunday
3 of Wands

April Tarot Spread

5
4
3
2
1

*New year potential
*How to boost your energy
*Fertile new growth you should focus on
*Suprises to look forward too
*How to navigate transformations

Hot Cross Bun
Tarot Spread

*What cross are you bearing
*What sweet things are coming your way
*Changes for the season
*Sacrifices to make
*Abundance & prosperity

Easter/Ostara Tarot Spread

5

4

3

2

1

*New birth energy
*Cracking ideas
*Fertile new growth you should focus on
*Abundant gifts coming your way
*How to smash through challenges

This Weeks Tarot Vibes

Tarot: 3 of Wands - 1-7 April - Astrology: Sun in Aries

This week promises to be exceptional, as you witness the realization of your ideas and inspirations. Engage in tasks that infuse you with excitement and determination. Motivate yourself to take action and actively work towards your goals. Be diligent in your planning and preparation.
In the realm of Tarot and Astrology, this week is marked by a compelling force that signals both success and adventurous opportunities. It is an energy that thrives on proactive engagement, making things come to fruition.

Mystic message:
Attaining positive milestones is a result of putting your ideas into action.

Manifesting:
When seeking tangible results from your actions, accompanied by the prospect of additional opportunities unfolding.

April Week 15

1 **Monday**

3 of Wands

2 **Tuesday**

3 of Wands

3 **Wednesday**

3 of Wands

4 **Thursday**

3 of Wands

5 **Friday**

3 of Wands

6 **Saturday**

3 of Wands

7 **Sunday**

3 of Wands

Tarot: 3 of Wands - 8th-10th April - Astrology:Sun in Aries
Tarot: 4 of Wands 11th - 14th Astrology: Venus in Aries

This week presents an excellent opportunity for experiencing success and a renewed drive to action, allowing you to celebrate your well-deserved achievements. Your diligent work and decisive actions may yield rewarding outcomes, such as job applications resulting in fulfilling opportunities.
In the realms of Tarot and Astrology, there is a sense of unity in the celebration of success. This week may also bring about shared celebrations with others, making it particularly favorable for events such as weddings and parties.

Mystic message:
Take the time to celebrate your achievements, for there is good news to be shared.

Manifesting:
This approach is ideal when seeking to manifest successful marriages and the sharing of significant rewards with others.

April Week 16

8 **Monday**
3 of Wands

9 **Tuesday**
3 of Wands

10 **Wednesday**
3 of Wands

11 **Thursday**
4 of Wands

12 **Friday**
4 of Wands

13 **Saturday**
4 of Wands

14 **Sunday**
4 of Wands

This Weeks Tarot Vibes

Tarot: 4 of Wands - 15th - 20th April - Astrology: Venus in Aries
Tarot: 5 of Pentacles 21st April - Astrology: Mecury in Taurus

While it is undoubtedly important to acknowledge and celebrate your achievements, an excessive focus on enjoyment and celebrations might lead to burnout and necessitate a more prudent allocation of resources. Be cautious this week, as there may be power struggles towards the end of the week.
In the context of Tarot and Astrology, it is advisable to gradually pace yourself as the week progresses, resisting the temptation to overexert, even if you are initially driven to do so.

Mystic message:
A new chapter is unfolding, and it may bring a dose of reality

Manifesting:
While it may not be the most favorable card for manifestations, it's essential to focus on the positive aspect of knowing that support is available if you seek it.

April Week 17

15 **Monday**
3 of Wands

16 **Tuesday**
4 of Wands

17 **Wednesday**
4 of Wands

18 **Thursday**
4 of Wands

19 **Friday**
4 of Wands

20 **Saturday**
4 of Wands

21 **Sunday**
5 of Pentacles

Tarot -5 of Pentacles 22nd - 28th April -Astrology: Mercury in Taurus

This week may present some challenges, although it's important to remember that these difficulties are transient. Exercise mindfulness regarding your health and the management of practical matters. Support is readily available, and you need not endure these struggles in isolation. Some individuals may find this week more challenging than others, so exercise caution with your expenditures.

In the realms of Tarot and Astrology, effective communication and clear thinking can empower you to overcome these adversities. Apply your intellect wisely in navigating these challenges

Mystic message:
Don't hesitate to seek assistance. There is no need to endure difficulties in solitude.

Manifesting:
Manifesting with this card can be challenging due to its association with potential losses. However, a more positive approach would be to promote communication and astute problem-solving in seeking help and support to navigate challenging situations effectively

April Week 18

22 **Monday**
5 of Pentacles

23 **Tuesday**
5 of Pentacles

24 **Wednesday**
5 of Pentacles

25 **Thursday**
5 of Pentacles

26 **Friday**
5 of Pentacles

27 **Saturday**
5 of Pentacles

28 **Sunday**
5 of Pentacles

May Tarot Spread

1

2

3

4

5

6

*What vibe does May bring
*What is coming into flower
*Boost to over come challenges
*How can you blossom in your own right
*What do you need to action next
*May Tarot message

Beltane Tarot Spread

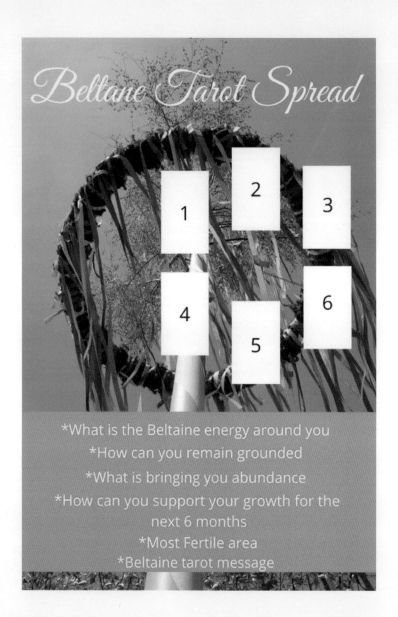

1

2

3

4

5

6

*What is the Beltaine energy around you
*How can you remain grounded
*What is bringing you abundance
*How can you support your growth for the
next 6 months
*Most Fertile area
*Beltaine tarot message

This Weeks Tarot Vibes

Tarot: 5 of Pentacles - 29th - 30th April - Astrology:
Mecury in Taurus
Tarot: 6 of Pentacles - 1st - 6th May - Astrology: Moon in
Taurus

We are transitioning from the recent challenges into a
more balanced and harmonious phase. This week offers
an excellent opportunity to assess your financial
situation and work toward restoring equilibrium.
Consider clearing debts and achieving financial
balance.
In the context of Tarot and Astrology, the prominent
influence of Taurus, the ruler of money and values,
suggests a focus on practical values and financial
matters

Mystic message:
Overcoming challenges with the assistance of others
ushers in a more harmonious period.
Manifesting:

Employ this approach when requesting a monetary
increase to achieve financial equilibrium or when
seeking a just and impartial resolution, particularly in
family or practical matters.

May Week 19

29 **Monday**
5 of Pentacles

30 **Tuesday**
5 of Pentacles

1 **Wednesday**
6 of Pentacles

2 **Thursday**
6 of Pentacles

3 **Friday**
6 of Pentacles

4 **Saturday**
6 of Pentacles

5 **Sunday**
6 of Pentacles

Tarot: 6 of Pentacles - 6th -10th May - Astrology: Moon in Taurus
Tarot: 7 of Pentacles - 11th - 12th May - Astrology: Saturn in Taurus

This week places a spotlight on values, finances, and material concerns, offering an opportunity for a greater sense of balance. You may find yourself questioning your values and considering where you want to allocate your energy in the future. As you reassess your priorities, take a moment to reflect on how far you've come.
In the context of Tarot and Astrology, the recurring presence of Taurus instills a sense of security, enabling you to refocus your ideals and gain a renewed sense of clarity in your aspirations.

Mystic message:
While your practical endeavors have the potential to yield positive outcomes, it's crucial to maintain patience as you work towards the ultimate result. Avoid giving up, but consider taking a brief pause to recharge your energies.

Manifesting:
When you are aspiring to achieve greater and more significant objectives, it is essential to allocate the necessary time for long-term success.

May Week 20

6 Monday
6 of Pentacles

7 Tuesday
6 of Pentacles

8 Wednesday
6 of Pentacles

9 Thursday
6 of Pentacles

10 Friday
6 of Pentacles

11 Saturday
7 of Pentacles

12 Sunday
7 of Pentacles

This Weeks Tarot Vibes

Tarot - 7 of Pentacles -13th - 19th May - Astrology: Saturn in Taurus

Take a moment to pause and reflect on your accomplishments thus far. Assess whether you are on the right path towards achieving your goals and determine if your efforts are justifiably worthwhile in terms of time and energy investment. Persevering with long-term objectives will yield rewards if you maintain your determination. However, be aware that this week may tempt you to consider a change in direction if you find yourself feeling unfulfilled.
In the realm of Tarot and Astrology, the current influences encourage the introduction of structure and security into your life. If these elements are lacking, this week is an ideal time to initiate their creation

Mystic message:
It's prudent to evaluate whether you are on the correct course or not. If you are, then continue with your current trajectory; if not, consider what changes you are willing to make.

Manifesting:
When it becomes necessary to exercise patience and perseverance in order to diligently assess the right pathway.

May Week 21

13 Monday
7 of Pentacles

14 Tuesday
7 of Pentacles

15 Wednesday
7 of Pentacles

16 Thursday
7 of Pentacles

17 Friday
7 of Pentacles

18 Saturday
7 of Pentacles

19 Sunday
7 of Pentacles

This Weeks Tarot Vibes

Tarot: 7 of Pentacles 20th May - Astrology: Saturn in Taurus
Tarot: 21st May - 26th 8 of Swords - Astrology: Jupiter in Gemini

The prevailing energy of this week suggests the importance of thinking outside the box, as failing to do so might lead to feelings of frustration and a sense of confinement. Always remember that your intellect is a valuable asset, and there is no need for you to adopt a victim mentality.
In the realm of Tarot and Astrology, it's evident that your mind is a powerful tool, capable of both positive and negative outcomes. Be wise in your utilisation of it to make informed and intelligent choices.

Mystic message:
Where there exists a strong determination, a solution can invariably be found

Manifesting:
Access your intuition and allow the symbolism of the water in the card to lead you towards discovering a more optimal solution.

May Week 22

20 **Monday**
7 of Pentacles

21 **Tuesday**
8 of Swords

22 **Wednesday**
8 of Swords

23 **Thursday**
8 of Swords

24 **Friday**
8 of Swords

25 **Saturday**
8 of Swords

26 **Sunday**
8 of Swords

June
Tarot Spread

1

2   4

3

*June vibe
*What need's your attention
*What's hotting up for you
*June tarot message

Summer Solstice Tarot Spread

2   4

3   1   5

*What can you do to be living your best life
*How can you bring more happiness into your life
*Where can you bring more balance into your life
*Vision of light moving forward
*What area in your life is about to heat up

Mid Year Tarot Spread

1
5
2
4
3

*Where are you now in relation to your goals
*What needs letting go of
*How can you bring back your focus
What have you learnt
*What do you still need to learn for this year
*What do the next 6 months tell you

This Weeks Tarot Vibes

Tarot: 21st May - 26th 8 of Swords - Astrology: Jupiter in Gemini
Tarot: 1st - 2nd - June 9 of Swords - Astrology: Mars in Gemini

Swords cards in the Tarot often signify concerns or challenges. This week, you are urged to apply your logic constructively. Seek methods to relax, reduce stress, and unwind. Avoid placing unnecessary pressure on yourself during this time.
In the context of Tarot and Astrology, mental obstacles might impede productivity. Nonetheless, by applying your intellect and ingenuity, you can surmount any challenges that arise.

Mystic message:
Failing to make prudent decisions could lead to a complex situation

Manifesting:
Take a moment to step back and contemplate strategies for relieving stress and anxiety, whether through delegation or meditation to calm your mind.

May/ June Week 23

27 Monday
8 of Swords

28 Tuesday
8 of Swords

29 Wednesday
8 of Swords

30 Thursday
8 of Swords

31 Friday

8 of Swords

1 Saturday

9 of Swords

2 Sunday
9 of Swords

This Weeks Tarot Vibes

Tarot: 9 of Swords - 3rd - 9th June - Astrology: Mars in Gemini

Worrying often proves to be an unproductive emotion, frequently giving rise to problems that remain unrealised. This week, as the saying goes, endeavor to maintain a positive outlook and seek happiness.
Discover ways to derive enjoyment without contributing to unnecessary anxiety.
In the realm of Tarot and Astrology, the current energy signifies the influence of mental fortitude and its transformative potential.

Mystic message:
Endeavor to refrain from exaggerating minor issues. Remember that challenges are transient, and a composed approach will see you through.

Manifesting:
Relax your mind by addressing one matter at a time. Utilise this card to assist you in setting aside your worries and apprehensions. Write down your concerns one by one, releasing them to the universe.

June Week 24

3 Monday

9 of Swords

4 Tuesday

9 of Swords

5 Wednesday

9 of Swords

6 Thursday

9 of Swords

7 Friday

9 of Swords

8 Saturday

9 of Swords

9 Sunday

9 of Swords

This Weeks Tarot Vibes

Tarot: 9 of Swords 10 th of June - Astrology: Mars in Gemini
Tarot: 10 of Swords - 11th June - 16th June - Astrology: Sun in Gemini

Recent weeks may have posed significant challenges. However, this week heralds a shift in the prevailing energy, allowing you to sever ties with past difficulties and bring closure to challenging chapters. It is crucial to embrace these changes as you embark on a new phase. In the realm of Tarot and Astrology, the influence of Gemini is prominent, emphasising the importance of clear and direct communication. Exercise mindfulness in your interactions with others this week, as you would not want to have any regrets about your words.

Mystic message:
Any foundation constructed on gossip will ultimately crumble under the weight of gossip. Exercise caution in your choice of words

Manifesting:
Allow the universe to show you what karmically is coming to an end. Use this influence to draw a line under difficult enedings once and for all

June Week 25

10 Monday
9 of Swords

---

11 Tuesday
10 of Swords

---

12 Wednesday
10 of Swords

---

13 Thursday
10 of Swords

---

14 Friday
10 of Swords

---

15 Saturday
10 of Swords

---

16 Sunday
10 of Swords

This Weeks Tarot Vibes

Tarot: 10 of Swords - 17th - 20th June - Astrology: Sun in Gemini
Tarot: 2 of Cups - 21st -23rd June - Astrology: Venus in Cancer

During this week, you are strongly encouraged to work in greater harmony. One door has closed, but it paves the way for the opening of a new one. Exploring opportunities with another person holds great promise. For some, this week might bring fortunate developments in the realm of love, following a challenging period.
In the context of Tarot and Astrology, this period signals a move towards a more harmonious balance, fostering duality and negotiations that draw you and someone closer together.

Mystic message:
A mutual attraction has the potential to yield numerous rewards.

Manifesting:
Utilise this card when you seek to foster a deep connection with someone, whether it pertains to matters of romance or business.

June Week 26

17 **Monday**
10 of Swords

18 **Tuesday**
10 of Swords

19 **Wednesday**
10 of Swords

20 **Thursday**
10 of Swords

21 **Friday**
2 of Cups

22 **Saturday**
2 of Cups

23 **Sunday**
2 of Cups

Tarot: 2 of Cups - 24th - 30th June - Astrology: Venus in Cancer

This week presents a splendid opportunity for negotiations with partners, cultivating deeper connections with both existing and potential partners. In the context of Tarot and Astrology, the prevailing energy is marked by a loving and harmonious atmosphere that radiates beauty and positivity. This partnership holds great promise, with Venus instilling sensitivity and affection, and Cancer, being the most nurturing zodiac sign, contributing to the bond's strength.

Mystic message:
This marks the initiation of a partnership founded on trust, compatibility, and a common objective.

Manifesting:
This approach is well-suited for both romantic partnerships and professional working relationships. Utilise it to promote harmony and equilibrium within all your relationships.

June Week 27

24 **Monday**
2 of Cups

25 **Tuesday**
2 of Cups

26 **Wednesday**
2 of Cups

27 **Thursday**
2 of Cups

28 **Friday**
2 of Cups

29 **Saturday**
2 of Cups

30 **Sunday**
2 of Cups

*Heating up
*What needs cutting away
*Love
*Friendships
*Tarot message

Summer Tarot Spread

*How can you shine your light to the world now
*What is flourishing for you
*Summer lovin coming your way
*What is heating up now
*Fun in the sun
*Summer vibes message

This Weeks Tarot Vibes

Tarot: 2 of Cups -1st July - Astrology: Venus in Cancer
Tarot: 3 of Cups 2nd - 7th July - Astrology: Mercury in Cancer

It's a time for celebration! This week is perfect for hosting a party, spending quality time with friends whom you share deep connections with, and embracing the camaraderie of your sisterhood. Revel in the good times, relax, and try not to take things too seriously.
In the context of Tarot and Astrology, socializing takes center stage, and gathering with friends, particularly for meaningful conversations, is emphasised.

Mystic message:
Savor the moments of joy and celebration; you have much to commemorate.

Manifesting:
Utilise this approach when you aim to foster celebrations, enjoyable moments, and strengthen your circle of friendships.

June/July Week 28

1 **Monday**
2 of Cups

2 **Tuesday**
3 of Cups

3 **Wednesday**
3 of Cups

4 **Thursday**
3 of Cups

5 **Friday**
3 of Cups

6 **Saturday**
3 of Cups

7 **Sunday**
3 of Cups

This Weeks Tarot Vibes

Tarot: 3 of Cups - 8th - 11th July - Astrology: Mercury in Cancer
Tarot: 4 of Cups 12th - 14th July - Astrology: Moon in Cancer

Seize the opportunities that present themselves. Following a week of high energy, you might experience a lull, so consider taking time to meditate and replenish your energy. Be mindful of excessive solitude or rejecting too many offers.
In the context of Tarot and Astrology, the combination urges you to monitor your emotions during the week, as they may become overwhelming at times, leading to heightened sensitivity. Be gentle with yourself and engage in activities that soothe your senses

Mystic message:
Immerse yourself in moonlight, practice meditation, and establish a connection with your inner self. Engage in activities that provide soul-nourishing pleasure.

Manifesting:
When you find yourself lacking motivation, employ this card to rekindle your enthusiasm and reignite your inner drive.

July Week 29

8 **Monday**
3 of Cups

9 **Tuesday**
3 of Cups

10 **Wednesday**
3 of Cups

11 **Thursday**
3 of Cups

12 **Friday**
4 of Cups

13 **Saturday**
4 of Cups

14 **Sunday**
4 of Cups

This Weeks Tarot Vibes

Tarot: 4 of Cups - 15th - 19th July - Astrology: Moon in Cancer
Tarot: 5 of Wands - 20th July - Astrology: Saturn in Leo

Exercise discretion in choosing your battles this week, as emotions remain unsettled. Be open to listening to everyone's opinions, bearing in mind that these are just opinions, neither right nor wrong.
In the context of Tarot and Astrology, potential restrictions and conflicts may arise among friends or colleagues, making it advisable to avoid entering into disputes during this period. It seems that people may not be in the mood to listen. Instead, use this week as an opportunity to gain a deeper understanding of human behavior and motivations

Mystic message:
Distance yourself from unnecessary drama.

Manifesting:
Utilise this card to enhance your comprehension of others. Observe the distinct clothing each person wears, symbolising their varying belief systems and levels of awareness

.

July Week 30

15 **Monday**
4 of Cups

16 **Tuesday**
4 of Cups

17 **Wednesday**
4 of Cups

18 **Thursday**
4 of Cups

19 **Friday**
4 of Cups

20 **Saturday**
5 of Wands

21 **Sunday**
5 of Wands

This Weeks Tarot Vibes

Tarot: 5 of Wands - 22nd - 28th July - Astrology: Saturn in Leo

Once again, it is of utmost importance to exercise discernment in selecting the conflicts that warrant your involvement this week. Not every confrontation requires your attention. Instead, seek peaceful resolutions and avoid unnecessary conflicts.
In the context of Tarot and Astrology, the influence of Saturn in Leo may present challenges to our egos. Nevertheless, it also has the capacity to fortify our hearts and refine our attitudes, ultimately fostering growth and enlightenment.

Mystic message:
Although the presence of competition and opposition from others can be distressing, it's essential to bear in mind that differing opinions and perspectives can also serve as catalysts for personal growth and deeper understanding.

Manifesting:
Utilise this card when you require enhanced clarity and a new viewpoint on a situation that is impeding your advancement.

July Week 31

22 **Monday**
5 of Wands

23 **Tuesday**
5 of Wands

24 **Wednesday**
5 of Wands

25 **Thursday**
5 of Wands

26 **Friday**
5 of Wands

27 **Saturday**
5 of Wands

28 **Sunday**
5 of Wands

*Holiday vibes
*Fruition
*Summer fun
*Best way to relax and recharge
*August Tarot message

Lammas/Lughnasadh Tarot Spread

*What abundance can you look forward to
*Gratitude
*What needs more growth
*Ready for harvest
*What is starting to change
*How can you maximise your skills
*Message from Lugh

This Weeks Tarot Vibes

Tarot: 5 of Wands - 29th July - 1st August - Astrology: Saturn in Leo
Tarot: 6 of Wands - 2nd - 4th August - Astrology: Sun in Leo

Following the conflict, the prevailing energy now shifts towards success. It's a much-desired week to actively pursue your goals, regain your stride, and revel in celebrations. Approaching challenging situations with fairness and maturity can earn you considerable respect from others this week. It's also a favorable time for exploring travel opportunities and reaping the rewards of your hard work.
In the context of Tarot and Astrology, take pride in your accomplishments and bask in the glory of your achievements. This power extends to those around you, promoting generosity, authenticity, and a sense of pride

Mystic message:
A significant milestone of positivity has been attained. Take pride in proclaiming how truly remarkable you are.

Manifesting:
Employ this card when you are in need of successful travel. It can assist you in reorienting your focus and manifesting a favorable outcome.

July/August Week 32

29 **Monday**
5 of Wands

30 **Tuesday**
5 of Wands

31 **Wednesday**
5 of Wands

1 **Thursday**
5 of Wands

2 **Friday**
6 of Wands

3 **Saturday**
6 of Wands

4 **Sunday**
6 of Wands

This Weeks Tarot Vibes

Tarot: 6 of Wands - 5 - 11th August - Astrology: Sun in Leo

This week promises a jubilant celebration of reaching significant milestones. Have you ever aspired to be in the spotlight, admired by others? Now is the time to adorn yourself with grandeur and shine as brilliantly as you can. It's a period of exuberance and confidence, a moment to persist in your journey with renewed determination. While you maintain your focus on the path ahead, take a pause to relish the fruits of your hard work.
In the context of Tarot and Astrology, a formidable force, akin to the life-giving rays of the Sun, empowers Leo to radiate as brilliantly as the stars, illuminating the way for all who come across its path.

Mystic message:
The universe bestows upon you the love and support of your fellow beings, who wholeheartedly share in your triumph.

Manifesting:
Use this approach when you aim to seize a promising opportunity that can lead you to success, reaching for the stars and illuminating your path.

August Week 33

5 **Monday**
5 of Wands

6 **Tuesday**
5 of Wands

7 **Wednesday**
5 of Wands

8 **Thursday**
5 of Wands

9 **Friday**
6 of Wands

10 **Saturday**
6 of Wands

11 **Sunday**
6 of Wands

This Weeks Tarot Vibes

Tarot: 7 of Wands 12th - 18th August - Astrology: Mars in Leo

Stay resolute this week, dear ones. If something is worth your commitment, the energy of this week will favor your triumph in that endeavor. It's a week to assert your stance and advocate for what you rightly deserve. While doing so, be mindful of potential jealousy and competition.
In the context of Tarot and Astrology, the prevailing energy carries a sense of heightened intensity, potentially even explosiveness. Nevertheless, it empowers you to assert your position and exhibit the courage to stand firm in your convictions

Mystic message:
Permit your passion to rekindle and allow your inner strength to guide your path

Manifesting:
Employ this approach when you find yourself in need of the courage to protect your interests and forge ahead.

August Week 34

12 Monday
7 of Wands

13 Tuesday
7 of Wands

14 Wednesday
7 of Wands

15 Thursday
7 of Wands

16 Friday
7 of Wands

17 Saturday
7 of Wands

18 Sunday
7 of Wands

This Weeks Tarot Vibes

Tarot: 7 of Wands 19th - 21st August - Astrology: Mars in Leo
Tarot: 8 of Pentacles 22nd - 25th - Sun in Virgo

By advocating for your convictions, you can redirect your attention towards more practical aspects of your life. This week is conducive to prioritising your goals, practical matters, and identifying what is truly worth your commitment. The prevailing energy encourages a shift towards a more meticulous focus on essential details.
In the context of Tarot and Astrology, it is a time to secure what holds significance for you and to enhance your focus on mastering the finer points of your ideas

Mystic message:
Consider consolidating your efforts and resources into a single venture, avoiding unnecessary scattering of your focus.

Manifesting:
Use this approach when you require a means to remain steadfast and in alignment with your goals and aspirations.

August Week 35

19 Monday
7 of Wands

20 Tuesday
7 of Wands

21 Wednesday
7 of Wands

22 Thursday
8 of Pentacles

23 Friday
8 of Pentacles

24 Saturday
8 of Pentacles

25 Sunday
8 of Pentacles

September Tarot Spread

1   2   3   4   5

*Septembers vibe
*Harvest for you
*Important question answered
*What to focus on
*Monthly message

Autumn Equinox
Tarot Spread

1

5

2

4

3

*How can you find balance
*What area needs letting go of
*What is changing
*How can you maximise abundance
*Season Tarot message

This Weeks Tarot Vibes

Tarot: 8 of Pentacles - 26th - 31st August - Astrology: Sun in Virgo
Tarot: 9 of Pentacles 1st September - Astrology: Venus in Virgo

Persist in prioritising your tasks and projects; your diligent efforts will yield results. Concentrate on completing your ongoing projects and organising your to-do lists.
In the context of Tarot and Astrology, the heightened energies of Virgo are at play, contributing to improved organisational skills and attention to detail.
Employ this approach to manifest success and material security, particularly in matters related to relocating or feeling at ease in your surroundings, even in foreign lands.

Mystic message:
You will begin to witness tangible results emerging from your diligent efforts.

Manifesting:
Employ this approach to manifest success and material security, particularly in matters related to relocating or feeling at ease in your surroundings, even in foreign lands.

August/September Week 36

26 **Monday**
8 of Pentacles

27 **Tuesday**
8 of Pentacles

28 **Wednesday**
8 of Pentacles

29 **Thursday**
8 of Pentacles

30 **Friday**
8 of Pentacles

31 **Saturday**
8 of Pentacles

1 **Sunday**
9 of Pentacles

This Weeks Tarot Vibes

Tarot: 9 of Pentacles 1 - 8th September - Astrology: Venus in Virgo

This week offers a wonderful opportunity to relish the rewards of your hard work. Treat yourself to something exquisite – you've earned it! Recognize that you possess the capability to establish your own security and should refrain from depending on others.
In the context of Tarot and Astrology, the focus lies in savoring life's finer aspects due to your dedicated efforts and unwavering focus.

Mystic message:
You don't require anyone else to make you feel fabulous; you are perfectly capable of achieving that on your own

Manifesting:
Utilize this approach when you aim to usher in success and bring about the fruition of your efforts, fostering the best possible outcomes.

September week 37

2 Monday
9 of Pentacles

3 Tuesday
9 of Pentacles

4 Wednesday
9 of Pentacles

5 Thursday
9 of Pentacles

6 Friday
9 of Pentacles

7 Saturday
9 of Pentacles

8 Sunday
9 of Pentacles

This Weeks Tarot Vibes

Tarot: 9 of Pentacles 9th - 11th September - Astrology: Venus in Virgo
Tarot: 10 of Pentacles - 12th - 15th September - Astrology: Mercury in Virgo

This week offers a favorable opportunity to reflect on your blessings, streamline your financial and household matters, and fulfill family commitments. Planning family gatherings can be an excellent idea for the week.
In the context of Tarot and Astrology, organisation takes center stage during this week, providing you with a sense of security and stability. This, in turn, positions you well to offer support to others.

Mystic message:
You have successfully achieved your financial goals and now have the capability to offer security to both yourself and those in your vicinity.

Manifesting:
Employ this approach to manifest success and material security, and to strengthen family relationships and ancestral connections

September Week 38

9 Monday

9 of Pentacles

10 Tuesday

9 of Pentacles

11 Wednesday

9 of Pentacles

12 Thursday

10 of Pentacles

13 Friday

10 of Pentacles

14 Saturday

10 of Pentacles

15 Sunday

10 of Pentacles

Tarot: 10 of Pentacles - 16 - 22nd September - Astrology: Mercury in Virgo

This week is an opportune time for getting organised with matters related to wills, family inheritances, and any financial aspects tied to family matters. Take a closer look at your investments, pensions, and any long-term financial connections. Prioritise family gatherings during this period.
In the context of Tarot and Astrology, focusing on organisation and resource management brings families together and fortifies their connections

Mystic message:
This card is associated with committed relationships, such as marriage or domestic responsibilities, that usher in love, abundance, security, and joy. These qualities benefit not only the couple themselves but also radiate positivity to those around them.

Manifesting:
Family relationships and ancestral connections. Use for success and material security that benifits all those in your home life

September Week 39

16 Monday
10 of Pentacles

17 Tuesday
10 of Pentacles

18 Wednesday
10 of Pentacles

19 Thursday
10 of Pentacles

20 Friday
10 of Pentacles

21 Saturday
10 of Pentacles

22 Sunday
10 of Pentacles

This Weeks Tarot Vibes

Tarot: 2 of Swords 23rd - 29th August - Astrology: Moon in Libra

The Two of Swords appearing this week suggests the importance of contemplating all possibilities and meticulously evaluating the advantages and disadvantages of various situations. Mental barriers may impede progress or the decision-making process. It is crucial to conduct a more thorough examination of matters before arriving at definitive choices.
In the context of Tarot and Astrology, this card underscores the significance of trusting your intuition in conjunction with logical analysis when faced with two or more choices.

Mystic message:
Occasionally, a stalemate situation conceals deeper complexities and intricacies than initially apparent.

Manifesting:
Employ this approach when you require the ability to transcend mental obstacles and tap into a deeper level of intuition.

September Week 40

23 **Monday**
10 of Pentacles

24 **Tuesday**
10 of Pentacles

25 **Wednesday**
10 of Pentacles

26 **Thursday**
10 of Pentacles

27 **Friday**
10 of Pentacles

28 **Saturday**
10 of Pentacles

29 **Sunday**
10 of Pentacles

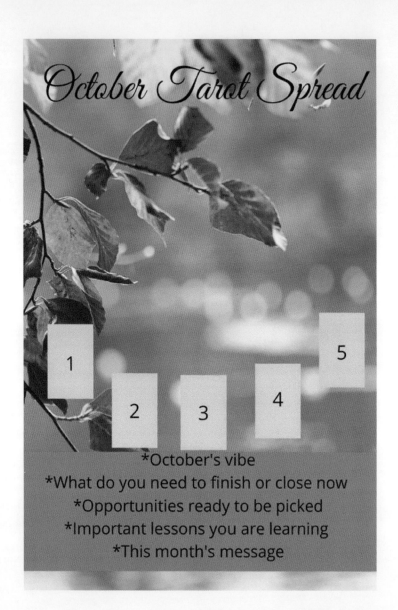

October Tarot Spread

1
2
3
4
5

*October's vibe
*What do you need to finish or close now
*Opportunities ready to be picked
*Important lessons you are learning
*This month's message

*What is the vibe you are attracting now

*What are the ghosts of your past that need to be released now

*What can you learn from your ancestors

*Trick to watch out for

*Treat coming your way

*What is being carved out for you this next 6 months

Witchy Tarot Spread

1 2 3 4 5

*What is bubbling away making positive progress

*Shadow side that is blocking you

*Pointed finger for focus

*What black cat luck is coming your way

*Witchy tarot message

This Weeks Tarot Vibes

Tarot: 2 of Swords - 30th September - 2nd October - Astrology: Moon in Libra
Tarot: 3 of Swords - 3rd - 6th October - Astrology: Saturn in Libra

Practice self-compassion this week and endeavor to avoid becoming entangled in emotionally intense situations. If you feel the urge to shed tears, use this week as an opportunity to release healing emotions, understanding that any difficulties will eventually subside.
In the context of Tarot and Astrology, the combined influence, primarily led by Libra, is poised to assist in finding a harmonious balance even within challenging circumstances

Mystic message:
Dedicate time to your own healing and seek methods to instill balance into your relationships this week

Manifesting:
While not the most favorable card for manifestation, in line with the current theme, consider how you can release emotional wounds and overcome emotional obstacles.

September/October Week 41

30 **Monday**

2 of Swords

1 **Tuesday**

2 of Swords

2 **Wednesday**

2 of Swords

3 **Thursday**

3 of Swords

4 **Friday**

3 of Swords

5 **Saturday**

3 of Swords

6 **Sunday**

3 of Swords

This Weeks Tarot Vibes

Tarot: 3 of Swords - 7 - 12th October Astrology: Saturn in Libra
Tarot: 4 of Swords - 13th October - Astrology: Jupiter in Libra

Once more, it is crucial to approach this week with self-compassion, treating yourself with gentleness and seeking activities that bring joy or add brightness to your life.
In the context of Tarot and Astrology, the prevailing energy suggests the presence of constraints and limitations, particularly in the realm of relationships. These may give rise to emotional obstacles or hinder partnerships

Mystic message:
Avoid involvement in troubled relationships or situations that carry the potential for hurt and pain.

Manifesting:
Use this approach when your mind is exceptionally active and you require a serene space to think clearly

October Week 42

7 Monday
3 of Swords

---

8 Tuesday
3 of Swords

---

9 Wednesday
3 of Swords

---

10 Thursday
3 of Swords

---

11 Friday
3 of Swords

---

12 Saturday
3 of Swords

---

13 Sunday
4 of Swords

This Weeks Tarot Vibes

Add Tarot: 4 of Swords - 14 - 20th October - Astrology: Jupiter in Libra

This week, it's advisable to prioritise rest. Whenever possible, take a break and put your feet up, allowing yourself to relax. It could be beneficial to make adjustments to your routine or allocate some personal time to reduce stress and rejuvenate your mind, body, and soul.
In the context of Tarot and Astrology, if your mind is burdened with overthinking, it may be time to take a mental break. Sometimes, a change of environment is all you need to alleviate the weight of your thoughts.

Mystic message:
Rest and recuperate, and give yourself a break from mental anxieties

Manifesting:
When your mind is overwhelmed with excessive thinking and worries, and you need to quiet your thoughts, consider how you can conserve your energy for more beneficial pursuits

October Week 43

14 **Monday**
4 of Swords

15 **Tuesday**
4 of Swords

16 **Wednesday**
4 of Swords

17 **Thursday**
4 of Swords

18 **Friday**
4 of Swords

19 **Saturday**
4 of Swords

20 **Sunday**
4 of Swords

This Weeks Tarot Vibes

Tarot: 4 of Swords - 21st - 23rd October - Astrology: Jupiter in Libra
Tarot: 5 of Cups - 24th - 27th October - Astrology: Mars in Scorpio

Continue to prioritise rest and recuperation, especially as the week progresses. It's essential to accept situations for what they are and adopt a 'glass half full' perspective rather than dwelling on the negative. Stepping back might have led to certain losses, but it's important to interpret them in a positive light.
In the context of Tarot and Astrology, this week might bring a fairly intense energy, and you may find yourself emotionally torn, inclined to focus on the downsides of situations. Nevertheless, it's worth recognising that things are not always as they appear, and there's a surge of positive energy on the horizon.

Mystic message:
Maintain a positive outlook on life. Exercise caution with any disruptive thoughts and actions, remembering that like attracts like.

Manifesting:
When you've experienced losses and challenges, employ this card to focus on the positive aspects. It serves as a tool for healing and a means to transition from dark times toward the light, drawing positivity towards you.

October Week 44

21 **Monday**
4 of Swords

22 **Tuesday**
4 of Swords

23 **Wednesday**
4 of Swords

24 **Thursday**
5 of Cups

25 **Friday**
5 of Cups

26 **Saturday**
5 of Cups

27 **Sunday**
5 of Cups

November Tarot Spread

1
2
3
4
5

*November vibes
*What needs your attention now
*How can you be healthy this month
*Best way to improve your finances
this month
*Action for manifestations

*Making a bang now
*Gunpowder plot
*Lighting your fire
*Blasting away what no longer serves
*Celebration
*Sparkling your way

Thanks Giving Tarot Spread

1 5

2 4

3

*Blessings you are greatful for
*How can you be open to receive more
*Blessings you have to come this season
*How can you show your gratitude to others now
*Thanksgiving Tarot message

This Weeks Tarot Vibes

**Tarot: 5 of Cups - 28th October - 1st -November-
Astrology: Mars in Scorpio
Tarot 6 of Cups 2nd -3rd November - Astrology: Sun in
Scorpio**

Seek out the positives during this week by creating a
daily list of five things you are grateful for. There's a
significant influence of healing from past emotional
issues during this time. Consider reconnecting with
people you may have lost touch with to aid in this
healing process.
In the context of Tarot and Astrology, you may
experience heightened emotional sensitivity, increased
intuition, and a deeper connection with your shadow
side. This week presents an opportunity to tap into these
aspects, while also using the light of the sun to illuminate
any shadows that may be blocking your progress.

Mystic message:
Adopt a 'glass half full' perspective and express
gratitude for the blessings that surround you.

Manifesting:
Utilise this approach when you seek to heal from past
emotional wounds and foster harmony within family
relationships.

October/November Week 45

28 **Monday**
5 of Cups

29 **Tuesday**
5 of Cups

30 **Wednesday**
5 of Cups

31 **Thursday**
5 of Cups

1 **Friday**
5 of Cups

2 **Saturday**
6 of Cups

3 **Sunday**
6 of Cups

This Weeks Tarot Vibes

**Tarot: 6 of Cups - 4th - 10th November -
Astrology: Sun in Scorpio**

**Reconnect with Past Relationships and Inner
Healing: It is advisable to reach out to old friends
and family members from your past. Embrace the
idea of forgiveness for any past hurts and work on
healing from any past traumas you may be
carrying. Spending quality time with the younger
members of your family or tribe can help you
reconnect with your inner child.
Tarot and Astrology: In the realm of Tarot and
Astrology, it's possible that you might find
yourself reminiscing about the past or
unexpectedly running into someone from your
past. Utilise the energy of the Sun during this time
to illuminate any hidden or unresolved issues and
replace them with love and understanding. This
can be a period of reflection and healing, allowing
you to address any lingering emotional baggage
from your past.**

Mystic message:
**Accept apologies, offer love, and extend
forgiveness in a formal and gracious manner. It's
important to acknowledge and appreciate sincere
apologies, show love and understanding, and be
willing to forgive.**

Manifesting:
**When seeking to heal from past emotional wounds,
foster harmony within family relationships, or
reconnect with your inner child.**

November Week 46

4 Monday

6 of Cups

5 Tuesday

6 of Cups

6 Wednesday

6 of Cups

7 Thursday

6 of Cups

8 Friday

6 of Cups

9 Saturday

6 of Cups

10 Sunday

6 of Cups

This Weeks Tarot Vibes

Tarot: 6 of Cups - 11th - 12th November - Astrology:
Sun in Scorpio
Tarot: 7 of cups - 13th - 17th November - Astrology :
Venus in Scorpio

It is essential to permit the natural process of healing to unfold. Doing so will grant you a fresh and enlightened perspective on your emotions, leading to a reevaluation of your emotional choices. It's crucial to maintain your emotional equilibrium, avoiding becoming overly disillusioned or overwhelmed, particularly when it comes to matters of the heart. This week is not conducive to making impulsive decisions. It's advisable to delve deeper and examine what lies beneath the surface. There may be underlying issues that require further attention before you can make substantial progress in your life. This introspective approach can help you identify and address any hidden or unresolved matters that could be influencing your current circumstances.

Mystic message:
when something appears to be exceptionally promising or too good to be true, it is advisable to conduct a more thorough investigation and scrutiny.

Manifesting:
When you find yourself in need of emotional clarity, allow your subconscious mind to connect with the subtle and unseen influences that may be affecting your emotions and decisions

November Week 47

11 Monday
6 of Cups

12 Tuesday
6 of Cups

13 Wednesday
7 of cups

14 Thursday
7 of cups

15 Friday
7 of cups

16 Saturday
7 of cups

17 Sunday
7 of cups

This Weeks Tarot Vibes

Tarot: 7 of cups - 18 - 22nd November - Astrology : Venus in Scorpio
Tarot: 8 of Wands - 23rd - 24th November - Astrology: Mars in Leo

Take the time to reevaluate your emotional needs, carefully considering the advantages and disadvantages will likely lead to exciting opportunities in the coming week. Be prepared to embrace these opportunities as they come your way rapidly and abundantly.
In the realm of Tarot and Astrology, expect an electrifying energy and a fast-moving pace during this period. While things may initially appear somewhat uncertain or chaotic, trust that they will ultimately align and fall into place. Stay open to the dynamic and transformative energy of the week, as it may bring unexpected but ultimately beneficial changes and developments

Mystic message:
Swift action prevents mossed opportnities

Manifesting:
When you are seeking to manifest and attract amazing opportunities swiftly, it's important to focus your intentions clearly and purposefully. To bring about such opportunities, consider setting specific and achievable goals, visualising your desired outcomes, and maintaining a positive and optimistic mindset

November Week 48

18 Monday
7 of cups

19 Tuesday
7 of cups

20 Wednesday
7 of cups

21 Thursday
7 of cups

22 Friday
7 of cups

23 Saturday
8 of Wands

24 Sunday
8 of Wands

*December vibe
*Gratitude
*Reflection
*Hope coming
*Tarot message

Winter Solstice Tarot Spread

5

4

3

2

*****

1

*What do you need to shut down that is not working
*How can you enjoy this quiet time now
*In the darkness what will shine light
*What lessons can you learn from this season
*Winter guidance message

Christmas/Yule Tarot Spread

*Gift to yourself
*Gift you can treat others too
*How can you bring joy to your life
*Surprise to be unwrapped
*What brings you abundance

This Weeks Tarot Vibes

Tarot: 8 of Wands - 25th November - 1st December - Astrology: Mars in Leo

It is recommended to take action towards what you desire during this week. There is a notable surge of positive energy available to revitalise your spirit and provide a wake-up call. This energy can be harnessed to facilitate transformations in the areas where you wish to see progress and action.

From a Tarot and Astrology perspective, the prevailing energy is characterised by fiery passion and an emphasis on taking action. Embrace this dynamic force and use it to fuel your endeavors, driving you towards your goals and objectives with fervor and determination. This is a time for proactive engagement and assertive moves toward your aspirations.

Mystic message:
Embrace the belief that there is a purposeful journey unfolding, and have faith that the universe will lead you to where you are meant to be.

Manifesting:
When you require motivation to initiate action and accelerate progress.When you nee to maintain a disciplined work ethic and organistion.

November/December Week 49

25 Monday
8 of Wands

26 Tuesday
8 of Wands

27 Wednesday
8 of Wands

28 Thursday
8 of Wands

29 Friday
8 of Wands

30 Saturday
8 of Wands

1 Sunday
8 of Wands

This Weeks Tarot Vibes

Tarot: 8 of Wands - 2nd December - Astrology: Mars in Leo
Tarot: 9 of Wands 3rd - 8th December - Astrology: Moon in Sagiterious

It is crucial to be mindful of your energy potentially waning during the week. Despite this, persevere and seek the underlying "why" in your reasons for coming this far. Discover the motivation that propels you forward. Make an effort to get early nights and rest whenever possible to prevent burnout and maintain your determination.
In terms of Tarot and Astrology, you might experience changeable moods and shifting visions. It's important to stay focused on your goals despite these fluctuations. Consistency and dedication to your objectives will help you maintain your course, even when external factors may appear uncertain or variable.

Mystic message:
It is worth noting that clarity is on the horizon, providing you with the capacity to perceive things as they genuinely are.

Manifesting:
When you require a reminder of the progress you've made and the distance you've traveled, while essentially to maintaining your focus on manifesting your desired endpoint

December Week 50

2 **Monday**
8 of Wands

3 **Tuesday**
9 of Wands

4 **Wednesday**
9 of Wands

5 **Thursday**
9 of Wands

6 **Friday**
9 of Wands

7 **Saturday**
9 of Wands

8 **Sunday**
9 of Wands

This Weeks Tarot Vibes

Tarot: 9 of Wands 9th - 12th December -Astrology: Moon in Sagiterious
Tarot: 10 of Wands 13th - 15th December - Astrology: Saturn in Sagiterious

It is important to persist in your efforts. You're making excellent progress, and even though it may seem like you have many responsibilities, the finish line is within reach. Utilise this week to gather the strength and energy needed for that final push. While the workload may be demanding and exhaustion could set in, make sure to allocate time for rest and recuperation in between your tasks.
In terms of Tarot and Astrology, expect a strong and concentrated surge of focus that will help you reach your milestones. This is a time to harness your determination and stay committed to achieving your goals. The powerful energy at play will support your endeavors and facilitate your journey towards success.

Mystic message:
It's important to remember that when you feel like giving up, that is precisely the moment to persevere and keep moving forward

Manifesting:
When you require the ability to manifest extra power and energy to complete projects.

December Week 51

9 **Monday**
9 of Wands

10 **Tuesday**
9 of Wands

11 **Wednesday**
9 of Wands

12 **Thursday**
9 of Wands

13 **Friday**
10 of Wands

14 **Saturday**
10 of Wands

15 **Sunday**
10 of Wands

Tarot: 10 of Wands 16th - 22nd December - Astrology: Saturn in Sagiterious

It is important to be mindful of the level of responsibility you undertake during this week. Avoid overburdening yourself and consider reaching out for assistance or support when needed, rather than shouldering all the weight alone.
From a Tarot and Astrology perspective, it's noted that there might be certain limitations or restrictions that impact your ability to enjoy leisure activities and fun adventures. To overcome these constraints, focus on completing your work and bringing order to your responsibilities first. Once the groundwork is established, you can then move forward and relish the prospect of engaging in enjoyable experiences and adventures.

Mystic message:
it's important to recognise that you don't have to handle everything on your own. Seeking assistance, collaboration, and support from others is not only acceptable but often a wise and efficient approach to managing tasks and responsibilities.

Manifesting:
When you find yourself overwhelmed and in need of encouragement to persevere.

December Week 52

16 Monday

10 of Wands

---

17 Tuesday

10 of Wands

---

18 Wednesday

10 of Wands

---

19 Thursday

10 of Wands

---

20 Friday

10 of Wands

---

21 Saturday

10 of Wands

---

22 Sunday

10 of Wands

Tarot: 2 of Pentacles - 23rd - 29th December - Astrology: Jupiter in Capricorn

It is advisable to prioritise what holds significance during this week. Carefully assess practical matters and make deliberate and well-informed decisions. You may find yourself needing to strike a balance between various choices, particularly when it comes to financial considerations, which might require some careful management.

From a Tarot and Astrology perspective, the energies are in your favor for establishing a more organised routine and structure within practical matters. You possess the capabilities needed to bring order and clarity to your daily affairs. Utilise this favorable energy to create a balanced and efficient approach to the various demands and tasks you encounter.

Mystic message:
Skillful management of resources, or "juggling," can indeed work in your favor.

Manifesting:
When you find yourself in a situation that requires making practical choices and managing resources effectively

December Week 53

23 **Monday**
2 of Pentacles

24 **Tuesday**
2 of Pentacles

25 **Wednesday**
2 of Pentacles

26 **Thursday**
2 of Pentacles

27 **Friday**
2 of Pentacles

28 **Saturday**
2 of Pentacles

29 **Sunday**
2 of Pentacles

This Weeks Tarot Vibes

Tarot: 2 of Pentacles - 30th December - Astrology: Jupiter in Capricorn
Tarot: 3 of Pentacles - 31st December - Astrology: Mars in Capricorn

This is an excellent week for fostering collaborations with others, uniting team players, and further developing significant projects to establish a strong foundation. Embrace a willingness to learn and make practical choices that involve teamwork and cooperation. Remember the importance of nurturing friendships in your professional endeavors.
From a Tarot and Astrology perspective, your focus will shift towards setting and achieving goals, reaching important milestones, and obtaining results. Being structured and organised in your approach will be key to your success during this period. Stay committed to your objectives, maintain a clear plan, and put in the effort required to realise your ambitions.

Mystic message:
it is important to emphasise the value of learning and growing together while maintaing a focus on mutual support

Manifesting:
In the pursuit of successful collaborations and when working within friendship groups

December Week 54

30 **Monday**
2 of Pentacles

31 **Tuesday**
3 of Pentacles

Monthly Numerology and Tarot Card Theme

Calculating Your Numerology Monthly Theme and Tarot Card

To determine your numerology monthly theme number and its corresponding Tarot card, combine your personal year number with the number representing the current month. Afterward, add 7 to this total. For example, if your personal year number is 8 and it's September (which is represented by the number 6), your calculation would be as follows:

8 (personal year) + 6 (September) = 14

Next, add the digits within this total:

1 + 4 = 5

In this case, your numerology monthly theme is 5, and the corresponding Tarot card is the Hierophant.

For the month associated with the Hierophant Tarot card, delve deeper into spiritual growth and knowledge expansion. It's a time to refrain from making significant changes and instead focus on establishing a more settled routine, especially if you've recently experienced chaos or disruption. This month offers an opportunity to return to a sense of stability and spiritual learning.

Daily Numerology and Tarot card Theme

Calculating your daily theme, personal number, and Tarot card associated with it based on numerology. For example, August is the 8th month, so the calendar month is 8.

Calendar Day: The calendar day is the day of the month. For example, August 23rd would be reduced to 2 + 3 = 5.

Add the Numbers: Add up the Personal Year, from previous workings out, Calendar Month, and Calendar Day. For example 3 (Personal Year) + 8 (Calendar Month) + 5 (Calendar Day) = 16.

Reduce to a Single Digit: Since 16 is a two-digit number, you reduce it to a single digit by adding 1 + 6, which equals 7. So, your Personal Day number is 7. The Tarot Card associated with "The Chariot" card in Tarot.

Representling focus, determination, and overcoming obstacles to achieve your goals. The energy of this card suggests that you need to remain driven and focused on your objectives, not allowing distractions or challenges to hinder your progress. It's a card of victory and success, indicating that you have the ability to overcome any obstacles that come your way. The mention of travel news bringing positive vibes might suggest that travel or a journey is significant in your day.

Number 1:
Characteristics: Signifies the beginning, embodying qualities of ambition, energy, determination, focus, independence, courage, originality, and a strong drive. It is often associated with the masculine energy.

Number 2:
Characteristics: The number 2 represents gentleness, harmony, supportiveness, consideration, sensitivity, tactfulness, cooperation, love, vulnerability, and sincerity. It is often associated with feminine qualities.

Number 3:
Characteristics: The number 3 embodies artistic expression, creativity, inspiration, imagination, youthful exuberance, confidence, optimism, enthusiasm, playfulness, joy, insightful thinking, and a penchant for fun.

Number 4:
Characteristics: The number 4 signifies security, a scientific approach, rigidity, structure, systematic thinking, patience, practicality, predictability, methodical behavior, excellence in business, and unwavering trustworthiness.

Number 5:
Characteristics: Visionary, spiritual, sensual, adventurous, explorer, constant change, dynamic, promoter, traveler, endlessly curious, insists on freedom.

Number 6:
Characteristics: The number 6 embodies traits of responsibility, nurturance, teaching, selflessness, love, parenthood, dutifulness, self-sacrifice, a focus on domestic matters, caring, sympathy, healing, and a deep sense of respect.

Number 7:
Characteristics: The number 7 represents wisdom, scholarly pursuits, analytical thinking, charm, studiousness, a scientific mindset, meditative tendencies, unwavering focus, introversion, the qualities of a hermit, and a penchant for deep meditation.

Number 8:
Characteristics: The number 8 symbolises visionary thinking, a strong orientation toward business, prosperity, ambition, a degree of control, a knack for politics, a history of success, keen insight, inherent power, and a natural leadership disposition

Number 9:
Characteristics: The number 9 embodies humanitarian ideals, philosophical thinking, idealism, a healing nature, self-sacrifice, kindness, generosity, a talent for writing, creative expression, artistic inclinations, and a sense of completion

Number 11:
Characteristics: Number 11 possesses the characteristics of the number 2 but intensified, manifesting as exceptional psychic abilities, heightened sensitivity, and a mesmerising presence.

Number 22:
Characteristics:The number 22 embodies the characteristics of the number 4 but amplified to an extraordinary degree, signifying an unparalleled ability to accomplish virtually anything. It reflects an exceedingly practical and methodical nature, often accompanied by grand and ambitious plans.

2024

January

Su	Mo	Tu	We	Th	Fr	Sa
	1	2	3	4	5	6
7	8	9	10	11	12	13
14	15	16	17	18	19	20
21	22	23	24	25	26	27
28	29	30	31			

February

Su	Mo	Tu	We	Th	Fr	Sa
				1	2	3
4	5	6	7	8	9	10
11	12	13	14	15	16	17
18	19	20	21	22	23	24
25	26	27	28	29		

March

Su	Mo	Tu	We	Th	Fr	Sa
					1	2
3	4	5	6	7	8	9
10	11	12	13	14	15	16
17	18	19	20	21	22	23
24	25	26	27	28	29	30
31						

April

Su	Mo	Tu	We	Th	Fr	Sa
	1	2	3	4	5	6
7	8	9	10	11	12	13
14	15	16	17	18	19	20
21	22	23	24	25	26	27
28	29	30				

May

Su	Mo	Tu	We	Th	Fr	Sa
			1	2	3	4
5	6	7	8	9	10	11
12	13	14	15	16	17	18
19	20	21	22	23	24	25
26	27	28	29	30	31	

June

Su	Mo	Tu	We	Th	Fr	Sa
						1
2	3	4	5	6	7	8
9	10	11	12	13	14	15
16	17	18	19	20	21	22
23	24	25	26	27	28	29
30						

July

Su	Mo	Tu	We	Th	Fr	Sa
	1	2	3	4	5	6
7	8	9	10	11	12	13
14	15	16	17	18	19	20
21	22	23	24	25	26	27
28	29	30	31			

August

Su	Mo	Tu	We	Th	Fr	Sa
				1	2	3
4	5	6	7	8	9	10
11	12	13	14	15	16	17
18	19	20	21	22	23	24
25	26	27	28	29	30	31

September

Su	Mo	Tu	We	Th	Fr	Sa
1	2	3	4	5	6	7
8	9	10	11	12	13	14
15	16	17	18	19	20	21
22	23	24	25	26	27	28
29	30					

October

Su	Mo	Tu	We	Th	Fr	Sa
		1	2	3	4	5
6	7	8	9	10	11	12
13	14	15	16	17	18	19
20	21	22	23	24	25	26
27	28	29	30	31		

November

Su	Mo	Tu	We	Th	Fr	Sa
					1	2
3	4	5	6	7	8	9
10	11	12	13	14	15	16
17	18	19	20	21	22	23
24	25	26	27	28	29	30

December

Su	Mo	Tu	We	Th	Fr	Sa
1	2	3	4	5	6	7
8	9	10	11	12	13	14
15	16	17	18	19	20	21
22	23	24	25	26	27	28
29	30	31				

2025

January
Su	Mo	Tu	We	Th	Fr	Sa
			1	2	3	4
5	6	7	8	9	10	11
12	13	14	15	16	17	18
19	20	21	22	23	24	25
26	27	28	29	30	31	

February
Su	Mo	Tu	We	Th	Fr	Sa
						1
2	3	4	5	6	7	8
9	10	11	12	13	14	15
16	17	18	19	20	21	22
23	24	25	26	27	28	

March
Su	Mo	Tu	We	Th	Fr	Sa
						1
2	3	4	5	6	7	8
9	10	11	12	13	14	15
16	17	18	19	20	21	22
23	24	25	26	27	28	29
30	31					

April
Su	Mo	Tu	We	Th	Fr	Sa
		1	2	3	4	5
6	7	8	9	10	11	12
13	14	15	16	17	18	19
20	21	22	23	24	25	26
27	28	29	30			

May
Su	Mo	Tu	We	Th	Fr	Sa
				1	2	3
4	5	6	7	8	9	10
11	12	13	14	15	16	17
18	19	20	21	22	23	24
25	26	27	28	29	30	31

June
Su	Mo	Tu	We	Th	Fr	Sa
1	2	3	4	5	6	7
8	9	10	11	12	13	14
15	16	17	18	19	20	21
22	23	24	25	26	27	28
29	30					

July
Su	Mo	Tu	We	Th	Fr	Sa
		1	2	3	4	5
6	7	8	9	10	11	12
13	14	15	16	17	18	19
20	21	22	23	24	25	26
27	28	29	30	31		

August
Su	Mo	Tu	We	Th	Fr	Sa
					1	2
3	4	5	6	7	8	9
10	11	12	13	14	15	16
17	18	19	20	21	22	23
24	25	26	27	28	29	30
31						

September
Su	Mo	Tu	We	Th	Fr	Sa
	1	2	3	4	5	6
7	8	9	10	11	12	13
14	15	16	17	18	19	20
21	22	23	24	25	26	27
28	29	30				

October
Su	Mo	Tu	We	Th	Fr	Sa
			1	2	3	4
5	6	7	8	9	10	11
12	13	14	15	16	17	18
19	20	21	22	23	24	25
26	27	28	29	30	31	

November
Su	Mo	Tu	We	Th	Fr	Sa
						1
2	3	4	5	6	7	8
9	10	11	12	13	14	15
16	17	18	19	20	21	22
23	24	25	26	27	28	29
30						

December
Su	Mo	Tu	We	Th	Fr	Sa
	1	2	3	4	5	6
7	8	9	10	11	12	13
14	15	16	17	18	19	20
21	22	23	24	25	26	27
28	29	30	31			

Kate May has left an indelible mark in the realm of mysticism, crafting a legacy of wonder for herself. Her journey began in the halls of Astrology, where she honed her intuition, delightfully guessing her friends' zodiac signs. Her curiosity took her deeper into the enigmatic realm of Tarot, where she explored the art of Numerology, the allure of Crystals, and the mysteries of Witchcraft and Spiritualism. Kate's passion for the otherworldly was ignited by her beloved nan, who spoke of the afterlife, thus sparking her imagination and propelling her towards her calling.

Today, Kate is the proud proprietor of the Mystic Coffee Lounge, a haven of magic nestled in her hometown of Cosham, Portsmouth. Here, she shares her mystical wares, including crystals, cards and gifts , and offers readings and classes to seekers of mystical paths.

Her first published oracle deck, Mystic Messages, is a whimsical and enchanting tool, offering direct messages of guidance and inspiration. aAlso available is her Tarot Astrology journal .

Kate has become known for her accuracy in Tarot readings, with many events foreseen through her intuitive gaze. Her passion for teaching has led her to create a foundational course in Tarot, catering to beginners, intermediates, and advanced seekers alike. She has also crafted an easy-to-download E-course, sharing her knowledge and abilities with seekers across the world. Thus, Kate's mystic gifts and teachings continue to inspire and enchant all who seek her wisdom in the realm of mysticism.

www.katemay.co.uk

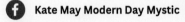 Kate May Modern Day Mystic   Kate May Tarot Psychic Medium

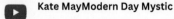 Kate MayModern Day Mystic   Kate May Tarot Psychic Medium

To order any of the following books or
Tarot decks or join one her courses,
contact her through her website on
www.katemay.co.uk

**Mystic message
Oracle Deck**

Tarot Journal

Astro Tarot Deck

Tarot Diary

Use this QR Code to gain access to Tarot Tips and Kate's Website including how to book her for a reading, blogs , monthly tarot scopes and courses

Link to Tarot Tips and Website

Printed in Great Britain
by Amazon